DATE DUE

APR 2 0 78			
FEB 1 2 75			

AGNEW THE UNEXAMINED MAN

AGNEW
THE UNEXAMINED
MAN

A Political Profile

by Robert Marsh

Published by M. Evans and Company, Inc., New York
and distributed in association with
J. B. Lippincott Company, Philadelphia and New York

Acknowledgments

THERE MAY be those who can bring forth a book such as this without any assistance from others. I am not one of them. If I could count all who played a part in making this book possible the number would easily approach one hundred. A few, however, deserve special mention. Miss Sally Nolan, who served as my research assistant, worked tirelessly and superbly in organizing and cataloging the information and interviews. Richard Levine's editing and stylistic contributions to the manuscript were invaluable, as were the final touches of my editor, John Malone. My secretary, Mary Lou Raines, served above and beyond the call of duty in the arduous task of transcribing the interviews. Likewise, the support I received from my partner, Joseph F. McInerney, and other business associates brought a necessary buoyancy to my efforts. Of special note are the mendicant efforts of Nell McInerney and Stephanie Nash, who nursed me back to health in the midst of the manuscript's first draft. Finally, I wish to pay tribute to the patience and encouragement of my wife, Susan, without whose devotion and confidence this work would not have been possible. To these and many more, my thanks.

Robert L. Marsh
Blue Ridge Acres
Harpers Ferry, West Virginia

Introduction

IN THE WINTER of 1970 I met with Vice President Agnew to discuss my plans to write this book. I had requested the meeting to tell him of the book project and to ask for his assistance in gaining the cooperation of those who had been closest to him. During lunch in the White House dining room, C. Stanley Blair, the Vice President's chief staff aide, did most of the talking, asking polite but probing questions about the book and the "position" it would take. In the course of my responses I explained as directly and candidly as possible that my purpose in writing the book was to give the American public their first real opportunity to know who Mr. Agnew was and why he was what he was. I added that I would attempt to do so as objectively as possible. At this the Vice President replied that he could not ask for anything more. Later reports from conversations with White House staffers indicated that the staff was "cautiously optimistic" about the forthcoming book and its treatment of Mr. Agnew.

Still later, after certain contents of the manuscript had been leaked to the White House by a high official of one of the publishers reading the manuscript, an abrupt chill descended upon all my contacts on the Agnew staff. Phone calls went unreturned, normal routine requests were denied and sources of information dried up. Agnew and the White House, it seemed, were no longer "optimistic" about the book. This development, of course, is not surprising. When the Vice President had said that he could ask for nothing more than objectivity, I was aware that he was responding like any normal, red-blooded American politician. He meant that he viewed the words "favorable" and "objective" as being synonymous. When I ceased being favorable, I was no longer being objective.

Needless to say, objectivity in such a venture as this is difficult. As the American public can attest, Spiro Agnew is not a neutral personality. In the course of the hundreds of hours of interviews and weeks of research necessary for this book, the prejudices and predilections of each source had to be analyzed and then placed in proper relationship to the events and issues that formed Agnew's brief pre-vice presidential career. Having known and worked with him personally, I had my own view of Agnew and the conclusions I had drawn in the course of this association had to be scrutinized and weighed.

I first met Mr. Agnew in my capacity as a broadcast journalist and later served as a member of his personal staff at the time when he was wrestling with the decision of running for governor of Maryland. I was with him when he made that successful race. Being with Agnew in the midst of the political maelstrom of 1966, working closely with him in a position of responsibility, gave me an opportunity to see him at his strongest (as when he denied a political future to one of his closest and earliest supporters) and at his weakest (as when he unnecessarily lied to reporters about a political assignment given one of the staff).

From these and later associations I learned that Mr. Agnew is not unintelligent, has a very deep sense of loyalty, an active sense of humor (especially when directed at others), is basically honest and is inordinately proud of what he views as his administrative ability. More important than any of these observations, however, was the discovery that the key to the Vice President's personality lay in his extreme defensiveness. Indeed, my first introduction to Mr. Agnew came about as a result of this very quality. During one of my local political-commentary broadcasts in Baltimore I chided Mr. Agnew for having the thin skin of a political amateur. Within minutes I received a phone call from him in the course of which he protested my charge and suggested that we have a meeting in his office so he could explain his position. In later months I learned that Mr. Agnew could let no criticism, however slight, go unanswered. What appeared to outside observers to be a desirable if occasionally vexatious combativeness was, in fact, a hyper-reactive ego defense mechanism which was and is always maintained in hair-trigger readiness.

Without question, Agnew has most of those qualities still cherished by middle America: loyalty, a capacity for hard work, respect for parents, and love of country, all framed by an Horatio Alger story. Regrettably, what Mr. Agnew does not have is a quality which most of middle America has without being conscious of it: an understanding and acceptance of one's self. The Vice President is as incapable of self-analysis and understanding as he is of philosophical commitment. If there is any sinister danger lurking in the man, it is here. He does not know why he responds as he does to such stimuli as wealth, fame, notoriety, status, flattery and social acceptance. Just as he does not understand why he over-reacts to all levels of criticism and challenges to his authority.

Spiro T. Agnew may, indeed, rise to even greater heights of personal and political achievement. But history will record that however much his life and personality may have been known and understood by others, to himself Agnew remained an unexamined man.

1 SHORTLY AFTER the delegates to the 1968 Republican National Convention had voted to affirm Spiro T. Agnew's nomination as Richard Nixon's running mate, the two candidates appeared together on the convention platform for the first time. While the delegates roared their commitment to his candidacy, Richard Nixon stepped forward and raised his arms high over his head in the wide dystrophic "V" symptomatic of the New Nixon. Spiro Agnew, with uncharacteristic modesty, hung back a step or two, his arms at his sides, smiling only slightly.

The average television viewer, not knowing the man's history, might have assumed that Agnew was overwhelmed by the honor accorded him; the watchfulness of his expression, however, suggested otherwise. Gerald Ford, the Republican minority leader of the House and convention chairman, took charge of the situation, grabbing Agnew's left hand and hauling it up into the air, at the same time forcing Agnew to take a step forward. As though suddenly understanding that the moment called not for modesty but for self-promotion, Agnew raised his other arm into the air and waved, flashing his wide public grin. Agnew had been in politics only eleven years, and had much to be modest about, but since self-promotion was far more natural to him than self-abnegation, he appeared only too happy to discover that his new role required him to assert his native aggressiveness. For it was only by the fortuitous application of this aggressive spirit that he had managed to reach the convention platform in this exalted moment.

His prior political record was not an imposing one. From 1957 to 1961 he had been first a member, and then chairman, of the Baltimore County Appeals Board (for zoning); he was Baltimore County Executive from 1962 to 1966; and he had served as governor of Maryland since January 1967. It was only a few short months before his selection as running mate by Richard Nixon that he had first managed to attract national attention, and he had never, during his eleven years in politics, been credited with any significant achievements, either in local or state office.

When he was nominated for the vice presidency, the aspect of his career that drew the most immediate interest of reporters from the national media was his service on the county zoning appeals board. Their hunting instincts were aroused. The potential for major corruption in such pedestrian offices is well-known to newsmen, and they swarmed into Baltimore County, Maryland, to ask probing, insinuating questions of anyone who would talk to them, from secretaries to local government officials. But they discovered nothing aside from a few stale, publicly known embarrassments scarcely worth rehashing.

Yet to anyone who would understand the making of Spiro T. Agnew as politician and man, the story of his service on the zoning appeals board is eminently worth retelling. In a public career as short as Agnew's, even his handling of the most insignificant office would take on added importance. But in Agnew's particular case, the years he spent on the zoning board are of special significance because they constituted his political testing ground. At the time of his appointment to the zoning board he was a political novice, and green indeed. During the next four years, however, drawing on his instincts and maneuvering to fulfill his own needs, he developed by trial and error his own very individual political style. Agnew did not learn his politics from the old pros who had run the county government into the ground. He figured out the game for himself. And since his way of playing that game brought him success—because he seemed to be making the right decisions as measured by his own political progress—his extremely personal, instinctive practice of politics became as fixed and as immutable as ritual.

What Agnew discovered about politics as chairman of the board of appeals, he used in very practical ways. He discovered a method of self-propulsion that served not only to satisfy his ego but fulfilled the additional purpose of attracting the notice and support of others. He used the method to become Baltimore County Executive. As county executive, he utilized the method to become governor of Maryland. As governor, he used the method to put himself in a position that made it possible to take advantage of the flukes of history (while contributing in at least some measure to the making of those supposed flukes) and gain the vice presidency. As Vice President, he is using the same method. . . .

* * *

In 1956, when he was thirty-seven years old, Spiro Agnew, having earlier dropped his Democratic voter registration, joined the Republican party. A struggling, unsuccessful lawyer barely able to support his wife and three children, he had moved his law office during the previous year from a cubbyhole in Baltimore City to Towson, the Baltimore County seat lying just beyond the city boundary in an unbroken extension of the urban area.

Up to this point in his life, Agnew had been unable to discover any path that might lead him toward better circumstances. Nor was his entrance into the world of politics an auspicious one. Lacking real political connections, even of the kind that are usually available to young attorneys ready to test the political waters, Agnew simply walked through the door of Republican headquarters and volunteered his services.

It was an important time in local politics. A special election was looming. In the November election of 1956, the voters had approved a new charter form of county government; it was to replace a commission government long outmoded because of the rapid growth of the county from a farming community into suburbia. The charter provided for the popular election of a seven-man legislative council and of a county executive to serve as chief administrator; it also sanctioned creation of many new bureaucratic positions in order to facilitate administration of the public services increasingly demanded by a burgeoning population.

For more than half a century, the county government had been in the hands of the Democrats. To assure an orderly transition, the Democratic chairman of the outgoing board of commissioners would automatically become the first county executive after the reorganization, serving a shortened term of two years until the next general election. Even though the Republicans would get no immediate crack at the executive position, they could at least challenge the Democrats for council seats with greater hopes than in any recent time. It seemed to be the year of clean sweeping, for some new faces with fresh promise. The county government was an entrenched Democratic stronghold; while it might not be possible to bring the walls tumbling down, there was a good chance to drive some deep cracks into the ancient structure. Community and civic associations had generated a great deal of enthusiasm for the promise of good and orderly government offered by the new charter. Much of this outpouring of nonpartisan political activism had been tapped by the Republicans and there was vigor and excitement in their campaign.

Agnew did not plunge in; he was too obscure. Rather, he slipped in, like any one of scores of volunteers with a lot of free time and a willingness to work. Friends of Agnew still picture him sitting for hours, addressing and stamping unsurmountable piles of literature or joining the brigades of door-to-door canvassers. During the business day he would call on acquaintances in an attempt to raise party campaign funds. He worked at everything, learning the importance of the inconsequential—the cumulative impact of stamp licking, poster distributing and telephone answering. He discovered that a person must often do a job himself in order to get it done. For Agnew, it was the elementary school of politics.

Election day, January 23, 1957, brought victory for the Republicans—a controlling majority of seats on the county council. Their terms would be limited to less than two years and they would have to work with a Democratic executive during this period, but they had gained effective control of their new government and, with that control, the power of appointments to reward their faithful.

Scott Moore, a leading figure in the party, and Gordon Power, newly elected by the county council as its chairman, both remember quite vividly Agnew's petitioning for a place on the three-man zoning board of appeals. Even though his chores had been menial, Agnew had worked hard. He had met a lot of people and he had attracted some attention. He seemed to have grasped the techniques of politicking and he was personally attractive enough to be encouraged within the party. His request was carefully considered. The party wanted to enhance the prestige of the board, which had become a caldron of public despair, a constant center of squabbles, politicking and charges of scandal or breaches of public trust. As a newcomer, Agnew was politically clean. He was also a lawyer, and the party wanted to have someone on the board who would be able to handle attorneys appearing in behalf of clients. The function of the board as an appellant body was quasi-judicial and seemed to call for the background and training of a lawyer. Agnew was offered the post.

Of the three members on the appeals board, two were from the Republican party and one of these would be appointed chairman. No sooner had he been promised a seat on the board, than Agnew impetuously began urging himself as its chairman. True, he had impressed the party leadership, but this was asking a bit much. Even with the most honest and intelligent administration, zoning matters were bound to remain controversial as the county underwent booming development. The chairmanship was too sensitive and too prestigious a post for someone as untried as Agnew. Not that there was any harm in asking. Agnew's boldness had paid off once and it was to pay off again. The chairmanship went to Charlie Irish, a successful automobile dealer and an active and influential party man whom Scott Moore and Gordon Power regarded as reliable, fair and impartial; but it was decided that Irish would serve for only one year and then resign from the board for a new member. At that time Agnew, after a year under observation, would be named the chairman.

It was a long year for the political novice. He had been generously rewarded yet he squirmed in this secondary seat. Very soon he was carrying complaints to Moore and other party members, usually in the form of criticisms of Irish, a man who lacked legal training and who had no knowledge of the courtroom procedures that Agnew felt would lend dignity and order to the proceedings. Perhaps Agnew felt that his complaints were properly objective and helpful to a party anxious to build an image of able leadership; but they were also self-serving, and decidedly pushy for a newcomer who had done little more than lick stamps to get on the board. And, in February 1958, Irish stepped down as chairman and resigned his seat on the board. He was replaced by an accountant, Charles Steinbock. Agnew accepted the gavel, confident that he would exercise better command than his predecessor and pleased to note that whatever the frustrations of his career as a lawyer, in the world of politics he had quickly been able to demonstrate his capabilities for the higher levels of leadership.

Everywhere across the country, zoning boards are nesting places for political opportunists. There is a smell that pervades such boards. They are the natural meeting ground of the fastest hustlers in the business community and the sharpest but least visible wheeler-dealers of the political machines; they present a situation in which both elements, commercial and political, can help themselves by helping one another. Even when honestly arrived at through strict adherence to stated public policy, a zoning decision has the aura of a favor bestowed and carries with it an implied indebtedness. A zoning exception can be the first and most vital step toward the amassing of a fortune, and board members who cooperate are in line for appreciative returns, sometimes in the crude form of sums of money in small bills, sometimes in the more sophisticated form of political or personal IOUs to be cashed when the need arises. A zoning board is perhaps the simplest, safest center of graft in American politics, and among the most lucrative—a fact made obvious by the extreme importance with which politicians view appointments to such boards. The desire to serve on such a board carries its own indictment as certainly as does a visit to a house of prostitution. Only one motive can be at work—unless one happens to be a sociologist.

Agnew was no sociologist, but neither was he yet a real politician. He appears to have sensed a different kind of opportunity available to him on the appeals board. Board membership, and particularly the chairmanship, could be a step toward a judgeship. Many times he had expressed to his friends a desire to serve on the bench, but it must have been clear to him that such an appointment would be a long time in coming if he had to depend on legal prominence, something which thus far had eluded him completely. Presiding over the appeals board, with its courtroom atmosphere and procedures, hearing cases argued by many prominent members of the bar, allowed him to demonstrate his judicial qualifications. He was, in fact, just like a judge. He had to be impartial. He had to snatch at the facts buried in the obfuscations of attorneys. He had to weigh the private rights and the public good. It was a training ground and could be a stepping stone.

As for the more traditional forms of self-advancement for a zoning board member, there was no public suspicion that Agnew ever succumbed to what must have seemed a tempting and painless way out of his financial difficulties in those days. On the contrary, when political and professional associates appeared before him, Agnew seemed to exert increased objectivity.

Scott Moore, who had been responsible for Agnew's appointment, appeared as attorney for clients with appeals before the board. He remembers in particular "a good case" in which Agnew ruled against him. Moore later appealed the case to the circuit court and won a reversal; and in Moore's view, Agnew might have seen the case differently if their friendship had not been in the forefront of his mind.

By the assessment of most observers at the time, Agnew raised the work of the board to a new level of efficiency and integrity. He took pride in his decisions, a craftsman's pride in his work. Associates recall that rulings of the Maryland Court of Appeals upholding Agnew's board often came down in language closely paralleling, if not identical to, the words of the rulings issued by Agnew.

Agnew clearly strove for, and achieved, an impression of nonpartisan fairness—even political aloofness—and integrity. And when he had secured that impression, he hugged it to his breast and ran with it, straight for the circuit court bench. He never made it, but the race fixed his political future.

Agnew had served as chairman from February 1958 to March 3, 1960, when he announced his candidacy for the Circuit Court of Baltimore County. He did so against the advice of his closest friends, including his political mentor, Scott Moore.

Running for the bench was not the way to get there. Vacancies were filled by gubernatorial appointment. At the conclusion of their respective terms the sitting judges were required to place themselves before the voters. The bar associations, newspapers, political leaders, and the public in general supported the view that all sitting judges should be returned automatically to the bench unless one was guilty of clear misconduct. To force judges to run against contenders for their jobs, instead of simply against their own records, was to inject politics into a position that should be above politics. But Agnew was determined to go ahead.

Since there was no judge Agnew could accuse of conduct prejudicial to his position, he simply set himself against the entire slate, hoping that he would prove more desirable to the voters than some one of them. It was an impudent and arrogant challenge to the individual judges and to a system that had the respect of nearly everyone. And it was hardly an appropriate move for someone wanting to make his way in the twin worlds of politics and professional law, where adherence to form, loyalty to friends, respect for the established order and traditional rules of decorum define the limits of the playing field.

But Agnew did not see the inappropriateness of the challenge. He had, in fact, been running for the bench from the moment he took charge of the appeals board. Within three months from that day he became embroiled in a public dispute that brought him considerable publicity and at the same time set an abrasive pattern of behavior that would make it necessary for him to move on from the appeals board to some other position. The particular case involved a junk yard operating in violation of zoning laws, and while it reflected no weighty philosophic issues, it was given a large amount of newspaper space, with Agnew emerging as central participant and, with the closing of the yard, as eventual victor. Other issues and arguments, tiffs and squabbles, with attendant name-calling and political infighting, followed this first incident, until eight months later the county council, back in the hands of the Democrats after a general election, began calling for Agnew's resignation.

It all made good newspaper copy, and Agnew proved to be first responsive to the attention, then enamoured of it, and finally even addicted to it. By this time only one other Republican held public office, a lesser one, in the county. Agnew's post was appointive, but nevertheless it made him the leading GOP officeholder in that narrow field; accordingly, he behaved like the party standard bearer, keeping himself and the issues he chose to exploit in the public eye.

Even at this stage in his career, he was aware of the value of the press. It was an awareness that was to grow in intensity and sophistication over the next ten years. Newspapers, especially, were a fascination. They devoted more time and space to each story than either radio or television; moreover, the printed word had a life span that went beyond the fifteen-second impact of a television news bulletin. Stories in newspapers were often followed up by an editorial, which kept the incidents alive and, if Agnew were lucky, fleshed out the bare bones of the factual account with a few accolades for his handling of the situation.

Agnew remarked at this time that newspapers were crucial to a minority party politician, who invariably had a great need but few opportunities for public exposure. Following his own advice, he generated a series of controversies, demanding, for instance, that the functions of zoning and planning be separately administered, and conducting a study of what he believed to be the excessive costs of zoning appeals. Armed with the thick pile of clippings that resulted from these activities, Agnew set forth in quest of a judgeship, against the mature advice of his mentors. With a splendid naïveté more appropriate to the hero of a fairy tale, some ignorant tailor or unloved third son in search of dragons to slay, he went directly to the county bar association and asked for its endorsement. The officers told him about the sitting-judge principle (which he understood) and assured him that they intended to continue in its support (which they did). They did not, however, take umbrage at Agnew for approaching them. His very naïveté, perhaps, protected him from censure.

He also went to the newspapers, seeking endorsements, but with better preparation. A friend noted that he had prepared for this appearance as though he were going to try a case. Members of the Baltimore *Sun* editorial page staff quickly informed him the paper was committed to the sitting judges, regardless of his own qualifications. Agnew, who had brought

along a file case, pulled out a list of instances when the *Sun*
had in fact departed from the sitting-judge principle to endorse
candidates it wanted to see on the bench. The editors were
impressed with this rebuttal and listened to Agnew's plea
for his own candidacy. In the end they declined to alter their
position and endorse Agnew, but they promised to do nothing
to combat him. Here was a rather formidable dragon that had
been neutralized, even if not actually slain. It was a lesson
in the value of direct confrontation with editors and publishers
that he would not forget.

Agnew did win the support of Republican neighborhood
clubs and of various individuals who had been impressed by
his work on the appeals board. He managed to organize a
committee of fifty prominent citizens who publicly urged his
candidacy. But he was doomed from the beginning. The election for all offices was a Democratic sweep. Agnew fell along
with the party, but the vote he received, although scant, was
not unrespectable for a Republican.

He had campaigned with decorum and neither the bar nor
the judges were unduly disturbed. Politically, however, he was
to be punished. The Democratic leadership professed to be
enraged. Within a month, rumors, privately confirmed, indicated the Democrats would get his head, denying him re-
appointment to the appeals board when his term expired in
April. Agnew professed shock that a party in power could so
blatantly retaliate against a member of the minority party.
"Agnew chastised us all in the press and burned his bridges,"
said one councilman. This was clearly an accurate assessment,
but Agnew was developing his own rules. With the help of
friends and friendly politicians he mounted a pressure campaign against the council. Letters in his support began appearing in weekly and daily newspapers two months before
his term expired. Community associations and civic clubs
publicly endorsed him. News reporters and editorial writers
then picked up the controversy and for two months it was the
principal topic in the country.

"He has established a reputation for being fair in all his
decisions," said one civic council. A weekly newspaper wrote,
"[Agnew] has established a pattern of conduct which has
commanded public respect for the board." In February,

seventy-one lawyers in the county signed a bipartisan petition calling on the council to reappoint Agnew. The Citizens' Planning and Housing Association added its powerful endorsement.

The county council, determined to perform the routine political beheading normally within its partisan rights, found itself facing a ground swell of public resentment, as though something reprehensible were about to take place. Dale Anderson, who would later suceed Agnew as county executive, was chairman of the county council during this overdrawn squabble. He recalls warning his fellow Democrats to reappoint Agnew, even before the public clamor began. "It was my feeling that we would merely make a martyr out of him," Anderson recalled thinking at the time, ". . . we would probably make him the strongest Republican politician that had appeared on the scene for many, many years." He may well have had that fleeting insight, but the record shows that at the crowded, noisy public session on the Agnew question, Dale Anderson nominated Agnew's successor.

Agnew did not take his removal with equanimity. The race for the judgeship had been a useful experience, but it was a caper that he had felt he could pull off without jeopardizing his seat on the board. Now it seemed as if he were back where he had started from in 1956. His frustration flared in his statement to the press: "The reasons for my removal given by some of the councilmen would make a new edition of Grimm's fairy tales. They are fantastic insults to the public intelligence. Such weak, small-caliber excuses hide the real reason about as effectively as a coat of cellophane. The job was being done honestly and with reasonable efficiency. Perhaps in the minds of some, those traits require immediate extermination." Nowhere in Grimm is it written, however, that he who tries and fails to slay the dragon may return to hang around the palace.

Yet this defeat, as so often happened in the course of Agnew's peculiar career, prepared the way for a greater victory. It is the primary paradox of his career, in fact, that nothing succeeds for him like defeat. His loss in the race for the judgeship (in which he never had a chance of winning) triggered his removal from the zoning board, and this action in turn aroused such public agitation that it was to establish him as a candidate for the office of county executive. If he had won the judgeship, or managed to retain his place on the zoning board, his career might well have been limited to that of a minor functionary. But by fomenting a public outcry at his treatment by the council, Agnew managed to engineer defeat into a thrust for higher office.

A few days after Agnew had lost his bid for the judgeship, the Baltimore *News-American* assessed the Republican possibilities in the county for the 1962 race, two years away, and found no candidates of any known stature. Agnew's name was not even mentioned. Three months later, however, after the council had removed him from the appeals board, the local newspapers began forecasting political repercussions that would project Agnew into the 1962 election. There was wide agreement, shared by the Democrats and by Agnew himself, that he had emerged as the leading Republican and as a growing force in county politics. In 1957, when he had sought the appeals board position, he had been near desperation in his quest for some form of personal achievement. Now three years had passed. He was publicly recognized. He had found something he could do and he was acquiring no small degree of self-confidence. So much so, in fact, that when a New York law firm invited him in 1960 to join its partnership at a salary of $25,000 a year, a considerably higher annual income than he was accustomed to, Agnew turned it down. He wanted to stay in Baltimore County.

2

ALL THE PERSONAL ambitions, hopes and desires of Spiro T. Agnew came to a glorious culmination when he achieved the vice presidency of the United States—and got to play golf with Bob Hope. There he is in the press wirephotos, his face frozen into a amiable big-fellow smile, not just brushing elbows with Mr. Hope, but as much a target of the cameras as Bob himself, his quips more eagerly sought after than those of the show-biz master, even though both use the same gag writers.

To tour the greens with the prominent comedian under the red eyes of network television cameras, exchanging banter within earshot of journalists from the nation's leading newspapers, is a sporty, casual symbol of having made it. It signifies acceptance by exactly the kind of boys Agnew has always admired: men whose well-groomed, well-dressed, manicured masculinity reflects a material success every bit as important as diplomas or family background, more important, in fact, to men lacking the other prerequisites of self-importance.

It has been said that the older a man gets, the farther he turns out to have walked to school as a boy. This small truth is reflected in Agnew's recent preachings, now that he has risen to the top, in his sermons extolling hard work, independent initiative and other spartan qualities not merely as an expression of American national character, but also as a personal credo—one learned, perhaps, at his father's knee during the bleakest moments of the Great Depression. None of these addresses itself to the problems of America as understood by directors of local poverty programs, mothers on welfare, black leaders, sociologists or big-city mayors, but it seems to go down well with the middle-Americans Agnew associates himself with; and it goes down very well indeed on the long walks on the fairways. Isn't Bob Hope himself an immigrant? And self-made? Isn't Nixon self-made? Isn't "self-made" exactly what America is all about? In fact, what were the Pilgrims if not immigrants and self-made? And doesn't that make a person's blood patriotically red enough and socially blue enough for any purpose under heaven? Once one is Vice President it ought to.

Agnew, in speech, manner, and attitude, has become the self-made man. He mentions his Greek parentage quite often, putting it forward as a credential for speaking with personal authority on the problems of minority groups. Not that he speaks of actually having experienced ethnic discrimination. In fact there is no American tradition of animosity toward Greeks as a national group, and therefore no reasonable comparison to be made between the experience of being a Greek in America, even a poor one, and being an aspiring black ghetto dweller, an American Indian, or a Spanish-speaking Southwestern migrant worker. Nevertheless, it is a comparison Agnew is disposed to make. Many Maryland Greeks are inclined to scoff even at his claims to "Greekness," pointing out that Agnew does not have his original Greek family name, cannot speak the language, and did not marry a Greek woman. Agnew's mother was a gracious Virginia lady, and her cultural heritage appears to have had a much stronger effect upon him than his father's.

The original name was Anagnostopoulos. Agnew's father, Theodore S. Anagnostopoulos, so the story, now folk myth, goes, arrived in the United States in 1897. He was penniless, and began his pursuit of the American Dream with a vegetable cart in Boston; eventually he achieved prosperity as owner of a Baltimore restaurant in the 1920s. The Depression reduced him to carting once again, but this time with a truck, and after another grinding climb he succeeded in re-establishing himself in the restaurant business.

Today Agnew speaks of his father mostly in reference to the bad years when he was broke. The impression given is that the now-successful politician had had to struggle upwards from impoverished beginnings. But the fact is that his father succeeded in the tough competition of the restaurant business not once but twice, and that he would have been considered more of a success than his son until the younger Agnew became county executive at the age of forty-two.

Born in Baltimore on November 9, 1918, Spiro T. grew up to be known as Ted Agnew, the last name legally changed by his father for obvious reasons, the nickname a further Americanization. Young Ted was never a very serious student, but after graduation from high school he was enrolled at Johns Hopkins University, where he hung on, in a chemistry curriculum, cutting more classes than he attended, until he dropped out in 1939. He seems to have experienced at that time a personal disorientation in the midst of international turmoil very similar to that afflicting American students of the Vietnam generation. Later that year he enrolled in night classes at the University of Baltimore Law School, where he demonstrated an immature and uncommitted interest in his studies and cut classes with serious frequency until the military draft yanked him away from his unscholarly pursuits.

In the army, Agnew was graduated from officers' candidate school and served as a company commander in the armored infantry in Europe. By 1945, when he was honorably discharged, he had acquired a Bronze Star, the nation's lowest medal for valor, and four battle stars, acknowledgment of service that would be about the average for a combat officer in World War II. Interestingly, his campaign biographies always omit his awards and rank at discharge in spite of the fact that such information is usually regarded as very important by politicians and people who write campaign biographies. Whatever his rank, his war service provided an opportunity for leadership and working with other men, and he liked the taste of responsibility and command.

In 1942 Agnew had married Elinor "Judy" Judefind, a chemist's daughter whom he had met while they both were working in minor jobs at the Monumental Insurance Company of Baltimore. By the end of the war, the couple had two children and were expecting a third. They returned to Baltimore and Agnew resumed his study of law under the GI Bill, meanwhile supporting himself and his family by engaging in an on-the-job training program as a law clerk at a weekly salary of $50.

His father offered occasional financial assistance and had

interceded with friends to get his son his clerk's job in the law firm of Smith and Barrett, two respected members of the bar. But in the highly competitive profession of law, Agnew's beginnings were not auspicious. He lacked family connections, social background and political friends; he had not achieved a high scholastic standing and would have the further handicap of a unimpressive diploma. The University of Baltimore Law School was a far cry from the Ivy League or even the University of Maryland. It was never accredited nationally; the caliber of training it offered was a source of concern to the legal profession even into the late 1960s, when the Maryland Bar Association threatened to withdraw state accreditation from the school. Added to these liabilities was the general assessment of contemporaries that Agnew, although hard-working and reasonably diligent, demonstrated no real flair or acumen. Despite this list of non-negotiable assets, Agnew managed to graduate and pass the bar examination, at which point he impetuously entered into private practice by himself. The experience was brutal and short. Scarcely anyone noticed his shingle when it was up or missed it when it quickly came down.

Agnew searched for a full-time job and found one as a claims adjuster with Lumberman's Mutual Insurance Company. The salary was $3,000 a year; he remained on the job for eight months. Meanwhile, through his father he had become friends with Circuit Court Judge Herman Moser, a member of the board of directors of a large Baltimore meat market, Schreiber Brothers. Judge Moser got Agnew a job with the company as assistant personnel director, a position that Agnew found to be challenging, and one that brought a livable wage of $5,000 a year. The company called upon his legal training in cases of shoplifting and personal injury, and used him in labor negotiations. The labor law experience was particularly valuable. Later, Agnew would be called upon to represent a labor union, Local 117, the Amalgamated Meat Cutters and Butchers of North America, and for the remainder of his law career he would derive half of his income from labor clients.

Agnew enjoyed the diversity of his responsibilities in working for Schreibers'. But in June 1950, a force of sixty thousand North Korean troops streamed over the borders into the Republic of Korea, and Agnew, along with other veterans of

World War II, was recalled to service as the United States began its police action in Korea.

Friends remember that Agnew, then thirty years old and with three children, seemed very bitter about this new military demand upon him and the interruption it caused in his life. He thought it an unnecessary and unwarranted injustice and began dispatching letters to ward off his recall. Although he went back into uniform for retraining, he was soon released, possibly through the intercession of a congressman for whom Agnew had worked as a campaign volunteer.

Having made his own separate peace in this first of the nation's brushfire wars, Agnew returned to Schreiber Brothers and his old job. But something had changed within him. There was an apparent discontent. His associates began to see him as hard-nosed, a martinet preoccupied with petty infractions of the rules. Agnew's relationship with the Schreiber management also began to deteriorate and soon both parties were racing each other for the privilege of severing their ties.

Agnew's employment with the market ended, but Judge Moser offered him a new opportunity, this time a salaried position with the law firm of Carl Steiner. Agnew did not remain there long; there was a stern discipline prevailing in the office and an atmosphere of close scrutiny—it was too confining. Once more Agnew turned to Judge Moser. The judge had been named chairman of a committee of the Maryland Court of Appeals to study the state constitution. Agnew was taken on as a research assistant. In addition, he arranged to share a small office with another attorney, Sam Kimmel, for the private practice of law. Most of their income came from title searches, for which they were paid $20 apiece. Kimmel recalls they were doing about ten a week and getting increasingly frustrated with the work. In his first full year as a practicing lawyer, Agnew earned only $5,000. His office was so small he and his partner were constantly bumping into each other; yet they took in a third partner. They began searching for larger quarters, but because the competition in the city seemed so overwhelmingly fierce, they decided to relocate in Towson, the seat of Baltimore County.

Baltimore City, rich in history, with its seaport and museums, has a population which is half black; a high proportion of those blacks are ghetto dwellers with marginal incomes. Baltimore County has a traditional foxhunt, whose hounds are blessed by the archbishop. Between these two extremes, in the suburban middle, Spiro Agnew was to launch his political career. Raised in the city, he had lived in the county since 1946. With the transfer of his law offices to Towson, the partnership seemed to find no greater level of success. Seeking other avenues of self-promotion, Agnew began to enter into community leadership roles, including participation in the county Parent-Teacher Association. And then one day he walked into Republican headquarters and offered his help.

3 BALTIMORE RISES in a natural amphitheater from an inland bay, the natural asset that fostered the city's creation. From this bay the land lifts and levels and lifts again; roads and valleys, like fingers extending inland from the waterfront, splay out in every direction toward Baltimore County, which encloses the city on all of its landed sides. As in all good American cities, the farther uphill one goes, the better the neighborhoods. The same pattern reproduces itself beyond the county lines; first the business, commercial or industrial areas, like a band around the city, then the suburban residential areas which give way to country homes, estates and horse farms in the beautiful interior valleys.

On March 18, 1939, the same month and year that Spiro Agnew dropped out of Johns Hopkins University, a country gentleman from the interior valley married a very good catch in the hundred-year-old, tradition-graced Trinity Episcopal Church in New York. The two events were seemingly as unconnected as a foxhunt and a restaurant failure, yet the two very different men who participated in them were eventually to have a great effect on one another's lives.

J. (for John) Fife Symington, called Fife, had been graduated from Princeton in 1933, the same year he rode his brown gelding, Palau, in England's famed Grand National. He had then traveled awhile in South America before settling in New York, where he was to start at the bottom and slowly work his way up the lower rungs of Pan American Airways executive ladder.

His bride was Martha Howard Frick, the granddaughter of the steel magnate, Henry Clay Frick. Marsie had been graduated from Foxcroft School and had made her debut in 1936 in

New York, in Baltimore, and in Pittsburgh, the city where her grandfather and other tycoons of the period had helped J. P. Morgan forge together U.S. Steel.

Fife Symington stayed with Pan Am even during the war, working in connection with the company's military contract operations while on inactive duty with the Naval Reserve. After the war he became regional manager of the Middle Atlantic states for Pan Am World Airways and moved back to Baltimore County with Marsie and their four children, taking up residence on a 505-acre estate he had purchased.

Now he was back to his roots. In 1948, he resigned from Pan Am and went into the building supplies business for a time. But primarily he led the life of a gentleman-farmer. He had the honor of being master of the Green Spring Valley Hunt Club for three years; the honor of being secretary to the fiftieth annual Grand National classic; and the honor of election to the board of directors of Baltimore Raceway.

Fife Symington also became interested in politics; when he finally gave up the building supplies business he claimed that it was because of the consuming demands of political involvement. In 1958, at the age of forty-eight, he became the Republican candidate for the vacated seat of United States Representative from Maryland's Second District, which included Baltimore County and two others. The Democratic candidate was Daniel Brewster, a man of similar breeding who used to race him in the point-to-points; Brewster, however, although only thirty-four, had established a reputation as a lawyer, served in the state legislature, and was viewed as one of the most promising of the young Democrats in the state. The *Sun* of Baltimore called both candidates "men of distinctly superior cut" (which was probably the last kind thing it would have to say about Symington) and members of "the country gentry."

As a candidate and as a politician, Symington did not let the label "gentry" prescribe his involvement. He engaged in politics on the level at which it was generally conducted in the county. He traveled the circuit of bull roasts (mainly hot dogs and hamburgers) , community dance halls, oyster roasts and service-club luncheons. He claimed his opponent was part of the county's Democratic "gang" tied by political manipulators and money-men to the "city boss crowd" in Baltimore; it was the kind of claim that led to his being accused by the mayor of Baltimore of running a "rough, mean and dirty" campaign. In fact, Symington was no rougher than might have been expected of a candidate running from behind in a jurisdiction heavily weighted in favor of the opposition party. And, anyway, the words rough and dirty might be used as basic terms of description in discussing the nature of politics in Baltimore County. The *Sun* thought Brewster was the better man and endorsed him. So did the voters. Symington got 55,700 votes to 89,900 for Brewster.

By this time Symington had become a leader of the county Republican party and was important in the conservative wing of the state party. Originally a conservative Democrat—he once described himself as "a Southern Democrat"—Symington stood firmly on the right edge of the Republican party. Impatient with Eisenhower, furious with men like Scranton and Rockefeller, opposed to federal aid to local schools, he was in 1964 the principal Maryland supporter of the presidential candidacy of Barry Goldwater.

In 1960, Symington once again ran for Congress against Brewster, now the incumbent, and lost again—125,900 to 88,100. It was during this election campaign that Agnew was running for judge. Symington, stumping church suppers and community hall gatherings, endorsed Agnew as a matter of course with other Republicans, at one point mentioning him along with some of the real party leaders as "distinguished aspirants." But it was not until the elections of 1962 that Symington and Agnew found themselves taking full measure of one another.

The congressional seat appeared to loom before Symington like a particularly vexatious hurdle. Despite his two defeats he was determined to run the course again. Brewster was vacating the seat to run for the U.S. Senate, and this development promised to improve Symington's chances. Agnew, intoxicated by the attention he had received while futilely attempting to remain on the zoning appeals board, had decided he would run for some office or other, although he had not made a real choice as to which one.

Apart from the personalities and ambitions of these two

men, the Republican party leaders in the county were excited by the prospects that seemed to be opening up to them. It looked like their year to bring in the harvest. The Democrats were hurtling into a primary election that was certain to tear them to pieces. Christian Kahl, the incumbent county executive, had served well enough to seek re-election, but he was being challenged by Mike Birmingham, the undisputed boss of Democratic politics who had once held the office and now wanted it back. The Republican party leaders—Scott Moore, Osborne Beall, G. Gordon Power and others—decided that they needed to find a good slate of candidates, avoid any primary fights themselves, and sit back and wait for the Democrats to chop one another up in the Democratic primary. Victory would then be inevitable.

Intent on his own rocket ride, however, and having no concern about his role in the party's future, Agnew decided to announce for Congress, immediately raising the prospect of a primary fight against Symington. Symington was planning a trip abroad before beginning his campaign. Hearing about Agnew's decision, he asked Scott Moore to handle the matter: "Look, get Agnew to change his mind about running for Congress. It's no job for a lawyer, anyhow, with a large family." Then Symington left for Spain.

Meanwhile, at a meeting of party leaders Agnew's name, as he hoped, was put forward as the likeliest candidate for county executive. And so the party approached him, asked him to run for county executive, promised him no opposition in the primary, and turned him from his feint in the direction of a congressional seat. But while the party prepared for a forceful, unified assault on the Democratic stronghold, Agnew, to judge by subsequent actions, must have been harboring his own thoughts, thoughts which had little to do with teamwork. Although he hadn't really wanted to run for Congress in the first place, it was galling to be told that he couldn't. Thus in the ensuing months, he would disassemble his own party, set Republican ally against Republican ally and emerge with a personal victory while the party went down to defeat.

Despite the excited publicity Agnew had been receiving, more experienced politicians such as Scott Moore did not see it as any guarantee of election, any platform to run on nor even as any particular qualification for office. It merely had given Agnew public exposure and the core of support on which to build a campaign. But Agnew obviously did not see the situation in this light. No sooner had he received the party's offer to be its front runner—a position to be savored in itself— than he began to expand his area of concern. He had no intention of following the safe strategy the other party leaders had blocked out.

His first move, in response to slights real or imagined, was a direct and insulting blow at Symington. Agnew encouraged George Arrowsmith, a wealthy gentleman-farmer, carbon-copy candidate, to run against Symington in the Republican congressional primary. Scott Moore went to Agnew, reminded him he was entering the primary with no opposition and begged him to stay out of intra-party strife.

"I pleaded with him," Moore recalls. "I can remember to this day him saying he never thought I'd come into his office and get on my knees and beg him to do anything. I begged him . . . all he could do was hurt himself, was my judgment, if he took sides. He was on the side of the angels; he had no competition. But it is not in Agnew to stay on the sidelines. He wants to be in it, and he got in it, and I'm not so sure it hurt him in the over-all picture. But it always seemed to me politically, the smart thing—Number One, don't have a primary if you can help it, and you can arrange these things when you have a small organization, but, if there are other primaries in other elections in your county, and you don't have one yourself, stay out of it at all costs.

"I was so, so positive that this was right I think Ted kind of—he kind of got a kick out of it. He just couldn't understand me, being so positive himself that he was right and I was wrong—and I'm still convinced that he was absolutely wrong on the thing, but I don't think it hurt him and that is the important thing."

Before the battling was over nearly everyone was forced to take sides. The Republican State Central Committee endorsed Arrowsmith, placing him on the official ticket in place of Symington. G. Gordon Power, who, as county council chairman in 1957, appointed Agnew to the zoning board and arranged for him to become its chairman, was now running for the state senate. The central committee had endorsed Power, but Power also joined Symington in a Symington-Power slate, a move that distressed Agnew. Slights against Arrowsmith now looked to Agnew as if they were directed at him. Agnew forced Power to clarify his position—was he or was he not supporting the official slate that included Power himself?

"It is with sincere regret and a sense of deep personal disappointment that I will appear before the state central committee," Agnew told the press. "For too long the Republican State Central Committee of Baltimore County has been attacked, harassed and divided by certain influential advisers who have historically treated the party as a part-time plaything rather than a solemn responsibility."

The committee meeting came in May. Agnew bore down hard on the man who had appointed him to the zoning board. Power was removed from the official ticket and another candidate was substituted, meaning that Power also would face a primary fight.

Power revealed his disappointment and hurt in his response to the committee. "How regrettable it is, in this year of unparalleled opportunity to elect Republican candidates, not so much that we find ourselves engaged in primary battle, but that there are those so desperate for publicity they seek to exalt themselves by downgrading others."

Power was now firmly in the Symington camp, but the fight he would face in the primary would take all of his attention and he would have no time to assist Symington. In fact, Symington would have to come to Power's assistance.

Agnew then began a second assault against Symington's leadership, this time concerning the central committee's control of party funds and their distribution. Agnew had no money of his own to finance his campaign; in fact, he was facing some immediate personal financial obligations which worried him a great deal. Facing no primary fight, he did not need money to secure his nomination; on the other hand, he could not afford to waste the lead time left to him before his Democratic opponent was selected in the primary. Political contributions were hard to come by; most of the money was going to one or other of the Democrats in the primary fight.

Until that fight was ended and its effects assessed, he could not expect to attract any substantial financial backing. His money would have to come from the party coffers, and as head of the county ticket, Agnew felt that his race should be awarded preference in the distribution of whatever funds were available. Symington argued that he had a better chance of election than Agnew and therefore should be allotted a sizable portion of the funds. As a result of this debate, Agnew began a fight to get his supporters on the central committee.

Symington may have felt he had a claim to the candidacy for Congress—by right of persistence if nothing else. But in making such an assumption and demanding first preference as party leader and county native, he could not have been aware of how the expression of his assumptions would stir Agnew's overpowering pride, triggering his instinctive audacity in such a way that the springs and cogs and flywheels of the party would be sent flying off in so many reverberating explosions, like some Rube Goldberg invention.

By now Agnew was spending as much time fighting Republicans as Democrats. This was not reasonable ambition. There are many words for the kind of excessive pride involved in such extreme behavior. The ancient Greeks called it *hubris,* a word whose implications Agnew clearly cannot have understood, in spite of the fact that he was capable of referring to "my ancestor Aristotle." *Hubris,* to the ancient Greeks, inevitably led to defeat, for it destroyed the balance and unity given to the controlled personality by the four virtues of courage, temperance, justice and wisdom. And defeat followed, so far as Agnew's immediate objectives were concerned. He lost out to Symington for control of the central committee, and both of his candidates, Arrowsmith and Parker, lost out to Symington and Power in the primary.

There was nothing to do now but settle down to the campaign for general election. The Democrats had followed the predicted course. Mike Birmingham won the nomination for county executive and once more asserted his complete control of the Democratic party. But the wounds were deep and his opponent, Kahl, released his supporters to go where they would. Many jumped party lines and publicly or privately backed Agnew. In June, Symington held a "Harmony for

November" party in his home in the valley; Agnew and Power acted as co-hosts, a visible sign that the Republicans were reunited.

Agnew was campaigning against the man he felt would be easiest to defeat, Birmingham, the machine politician. The Democratic split resulted in financial support and votes for Agnew. The daily newspapers endorsed him. In November, he was elected county executive by a vote of 78,700 to 61,300. But Symington was defeated, Power was defeated, and only one Republican was elected to both the county council and the state House of Delegates. The Republicans, at their time for harvest, had been denied once more.

Agnew and Symington would clash again over the next few years, with such frequency, in fact, that the relationship would be commonly described as a feud. But never again would the feuding be so lacking in substance, so clearly vindictive, as during this first serious political testing of Agnew when he publicly succumbed to *hubris* for the first, but certainly not the last, time.

In the election of 1968, Symington, a long-time Nixon admirer (unlike Agnew, for whom Nixon originally was a second, or even third choice), became Maryland financial co-chairman for the Nixon-Agnew campaign. His reward was the ambassadorship to Trinidad and Tobago, the islands off Venezuela. And there he presides, swimming in his sunglasses and wide-brimmed hat to protect him from a strong sun that he cannot stand, and driving each day to his office in Port-of-Spain where a portrait of Agnew, autographed, graces the wall.

4 W H E N A G N E W R A N for the office of county executive he had behind him a fumbling legal career made dreary with insurance claims, title searches and pick-up jobs with labor unions—a career on the fringes, considerably removed from that prestigious center where the best of the profession parry and thrust and win honor. He had served on the zoning board, an important and honorable place to be if one is honorable, and a rich trough in which to grub and root if one is not, but still far from the white-hot center of political power and glory.

Now, principally because he was a grandstander, because within him there was some compulsive urge to rip and tear, to publicly abuse and humiliate, to overpower with his quirky, saturation-bombing rhetoric, he had become a public figure. He was acknowledged as such by political colleagues who appraise a candidate according to how well he might run and care not a bit about how well he might serve; and by the press, so self-conscious, even guilty, about their own greediness to milk a political exhibitionist that they close their eyes to obvious public pandering, taking no note of it when assessing the attributes a man might bring to public office.

"He was a runner," Scott Moore says. "He was ambitious and he wanted to get ahead, and he saw this as a good way to do it." When the cocky, scrawny youngster takes the initiative to walk over to the dugout, or to the scrimmage line, or the piano, it is required by the dictates of the Great American Dream, as well as by all those Hollywood movies Agnew's generation remembers, that the next line in the scenario read, "Here, kid, let's see what you can do." As a lifelong Republican and a county party leader, Moore wanted a winner for his party. He had known Agnew since 1958 and felt that he had found a winner in his friend.

Agnew, however, ran his own campaign, not hesitating to reject the advice of Scott Moore and other experienced politicians. Putting into practice the lessons he had learned in the campaigns of 1957 and 1960, he analyzed his own and the opposition's strengths and weaknesses. He knew from the beginning that he wanted to run against Mike Birmingham, and the Democratic primary voters considerately gave him his choice. He began hunting around for issues and put together an eight-point platform, including planks on tax reform and industrial development specifically designed to attract the support of the Baltimore *Sun* papers.

Many of the community associations and citizens groups which had been angered by his treatment at the hands of the county council were influential and active in their own localities. Agnew drew on them for more support. Citizens for Agnew, Democrats for Agnew, and other ad hoc groups sprung up under his urging and guidance.

Before an audience, Agnew had a straightforward manner that got across to people. His speeches were filled with issue-oriented references that masked his lack of knowledge about the county and its government. No one paid attention to the meaningless generalities and simplistic solutions that he carried from one speaking engagement to another. Agnew has a knack for retaining facts and figures and an ability to recall them easily—a facility which impressed all his early associates, and later Nixon himself in their first meetings. During the 1962 campaign, Agnew found it useful to splatter his speeches and off-the-cuff remarks with statistics and isolated specifics which audiences mistook for knowledge.

Joe Pokorny, a law associate, recalls Agnew's anxiety the first time he had to appear at a candidates meeting. He was especially concerned about questions from the audience. But after the meeting, he told Pokorny, "It's so easy. And I watched an old campaigner like Chris [Kahl] stammer and stutter over these fielding questions. And I watched a campaigner like [Mike] Birmingham louse it up. . . . It's so easy." Pokorny adds, "This is the biggest problem he had to overcome, and then, when he got that confidence, he was fine." He became so confident and relaxed on the stage, and so disdainful of his opponents, that when Mike Birmingham emerged as the victor of the Democratic primary, Agnew began a persistent campaign to draw him into public debate. Birmingham did his best to avoid Agnew. As the candidate of the dominant party, he wanted to prevent Agnew from using him to capture attention. He was a poor public speaker and realized it; he was old and his infirmity showed. Everything Birmingham knew about himself Agnew knew also and used against him. He very quickly turned Birmingham's reluctance to debate into a campaign issue in itself. Birmingham could not escape Agnew completely, and when the two men did find themselves on the same platform, Agnew used his wit, his gymnastic vocabulary and his store of statistics and data to carry off each performance.

All of this hard work and planning, the newness of being an important candidate in an important campaign and his own development as a campaigner obscured the dominant factors in the election. The issue, after the Democratic primary, was simple: Did voters want to put an ancient, malodorous political machine in charge of the new charter government they had just initiated? Agnew was to be the fortunate beneficiary of a voters revolt. It was not his own performances that were going to give him the election; changing social and political attitudes would do that. His appearances as a campaigner simply gave the voters, already determined to defeat Birmingham, an opportunity to have a look at the new county executive before his election.

The breakup of the machine, which by this time had become inevitable, had begun with the population increase in the county after World War II. Chris Kahl describes the machine's troubles as follows:

> A lot of new people moved into Baltimore County who were a different breed than the old dyed-in-the-wool organization-type Democrat who did exactly what the Boss told him to do, or the local precinct leader told him to do. Yearly, we had an increasingly large number of independent people who registered Democratic, perhaps because we were the majority party and you might want a favor someday, or because they just felt that it was the

right thing to do [because they] came out of Baltimore City or elsewhere where at that point the Democratic party controlled.

But they were not the kind of voters you controlled as you controlled the old-time full-timers. We used to be able to say that the trash collector in a certain precinct in Essex was on our side; we knew we were going to carry that precinct because he had so much influence, doing favors when he collected the trash. Like you wanted a big stove moved, or an old refrigerator hauled out of the house or something; this was not part of his job, but this was his political strength—muscles. Then he could come back election time and say, "Look, you appreciate what I've been doing for you, you can keep me in my job by voting for my friends. Here they are, and I'll be around election day to take you to the polls."

Ted had going for him, of course, the fact that the old gang had been in power for years in the county [and was] full of corruption and what-not, and here's a new shiny "bright" on the other side offering you something new and different.

And when you get into the general election campaign, I think "old versus new" is a pretty good way to put it. . . . Here was a young man, yes; an aggressive candidate; an articulate candidate which Mike Birmingham was not —he was not very articulate, he relied on organization— and a man who was challenging in saying, "Well, come on. Let's talk about the issues of the campaign." And Birmingham just wouldn't show up and do it.

The general belief after the election was that Kahl himself had made the difference, tipping the scale in Agnew's favor after losing the Democratic primary to Birmingham. Kahl affects a certain modesty about his role, but beneath his disclaimers lies the key to Agnew's victory. Kahl and Birmingham had opposed each other in elections dating back to 1938. In 1958, Birmingham decided he himself had no chance at the polls and offered to support Kahl for county executive. Kahl says Birmingham asked nothing in exchange for the support, but when Kahl won he found that Birmingham expected to run the county. "He thought he was buying himself a muldoon, a guy who would hold a rubber stamp in his hand and say 'Okay.' . . . He should have known me better than that." The intra-party fight between the two men continued into 1962. Kahl says now that Birmingham tried to find some other candidate to oppose Kahl in the primary, but, failing that, ran against Kahl himself. Thus when Kahl was defeated he felt no allegiance to Birmingham.

This is the impression, certainly, that is widespread, that the cause of [Agnew's] victory was the support he got from friends of mine. Personally, I'm in no position to confirm that that is true, because he won by a very, very substantial majority. Now, I don't think there's any question that the fact that some of my friends elected to support Ted helped him. Whether it made the difference, I couldn't honestly say. He was a very good candidate. I'll say this: Ted could probably not have won against a united Democratic party. . . .

I did not take a position myself, in favor of Ted or his opposer. My friends came to me, a number of them, loyal people . . . there are a certain number of people in the world who have some sense of loyalty, who will stick with you, and that type came to me and, in effect, said, "Well now, what are we going to do, Chris? What do you have in mind? What do you want me to do? You know I'm your friend; I appreciated it, being on your ticket— if they were—or working for—if they had." And my standard response was pretty much to this effect: "I'm a loser, now, and I can't help you. But I appreciate all the loyalty you have given me in the past. But you do your own arithmetic. Do what you think is best for you." And in some cases, these people went with Birmingham. In other cases, they went with Ted. But they made their own choices.

I get the credit, to some extent, because, as people have said, if I had not released them from their obligation to me, and [if I had] said, "No, fellows, I want you to vote for Mike Birmingham, work for Mike Birmingham, because he's the Democratic nominee," then the united Democratic party would have licked Agnew.

And so, with Republicans, independents and Kahl's supporters Agnew had votes enough to win—78,738 to 61,313 for Birmingham. Agnew took it as a very personal victory and he waved his triumph like a banner. He had done it, he himself. Repeatedly, he told aides and reporters who questioned him during his administration that it was he, Agnew, who had won the election, not them. Shortly after taking office, he began insisting that his staff and advisers present him only with unvarnished facts; he did not need their opinions or recommendations. He had proved to himself the value of his own judgments and the strength of his decision-making powers. He paid off his indebtedness to those who helped him—even Chris Kahl received patronage positions—but he could not bring himself to give his supporters real credit for the victory. Winning was too personal a thing to share, as if he had been elected not in the political sense but in the Calvinistic sense of special election, of predestination.

At last he was his own man; and the change had come none too soon. During the race for county executive, Ed Hardesty, one of Agnew's law partners, walked by Agnew's office door one morning and saw him, elbows on his desk, forehead braced in both hands, face cast down. "What's the matter?" Hardesty asked. Agnew called Hardesty in and told him to close the door behind him. "My God, I don't know what I am going to do," he told Hardesty. He explained that he had just purchased a new house, had just signed a lease for the law office with a crushingly high rental over the coming ten years, and that he had other pressing financial obligations, to say nothing of campaign bills piling up around his ears. He could see no way out.

That had always been the plight of the early Agnew, deep in money problems with no foreseeable letup. The election was a help. The salary for county executive was $22,500. But Scott Moore still had to give Agnew money during the coming years as he attempted to bridge one financial crisis after another. In addition, with the office and its conspicuous display of power came the necessity to live on a more fitting (expensive) level and to maintain an image of financial comfort if not affluence. In all other ways, however, he had achieved his independence. An associate remembers that the year before, when running for the circuit court judgeship, Agnew had said, "Now I am no longer just a hack lawyer to the bluebloods." That race, he felt, had gained him new stature not only with the politicians but with the legal fraternity. But the accrual of real importance came with his election to the office of Baltimore County Executive. For the first time, it could be said that he had surpassed the success that his father had achieved for himself. He rode around in a chauffeur-driven automobile, accompanied by a squad of aides and retainers; he had scores of public employees to do his bidding; his favor was sought by hundreds—literally hundreds—of people; he found himself being entertained by the wealthiest businessmen in the community. It was the turning point in his life. Except for the one crack left by his continuing financial problems, he had sealed off his drab early life forever. And he was not deceiving himself about the change in his condition. Others took note of it, too.

I. Harold (Bud) Hammerman II was chairman of the board and president of S. L. Hammerman Organization, Inc., a national mortgage bankers firm established by his father. He was one of the men Scott Moore had gone to see about campaign contributions for Agnew.

"He owned a big office building and, in fact, Ted was renting from him," Scott Moore says. "I was renting from him, too. And I knew him and I went in to see him and ask for a contribution. He turned me down cold and said that Mike Birmingham was one of his dearest friends and one of his father's dearest friends. And lo and behold, behind Bud in his office there was a picture of Mike Birmingham. So I didn't get a nickel out of him."

But the circle of the elect in Baltimore County is small. And one of the businessmen Agnew was soon close to was Bud Hammerman. A mortgage banker, investor and developer such as Hammerman had to be close to whoever was county executive. When Agnew ran for governor, Hammerman became one of his big money raisers.

In 1967 one of the monied-men close to Agnew said that he was sure Agnew would run for re-election as governor (this was before Nixon called) "because he likes to ride around in the private planes of companies, and likes to be chauffeured around, and likes to get on the phone and call big shots." And those are the things he first became able to do when he was elected county executive.

5

$\mathbf{A}$ G N E W   S P E N T   T H E first six months of his term as county executive mastering the bureaucratic intricacies of local government, and worked hard to implement his campaign promises. Things seemed to be progressing smoothly for him, but then, abruptly, he was faced with the first of several civil rights crises that were to develop while he was serving as county executive and later as governor. On July 4, 1963, a major civil rights demonstration was mounted at a privately owned sixty-eight-acre amusement park called Gwynn Oak, located in the western part of the county near the Baltimore City line. In the following few days, Agnew became more and more involved in the problems brought on by the demonstration. Present in this first confrontation were all the Agnew hallmarks of later ones: his glib expressions of a desire to see an end to racial injustice; his contradictory unwillingness to use the power and prestige of his office to help achieve that end; his disapproval of civil rights demonstrations as such, however nonviolent they might be; his personal distaste for civil rights leaders; his inability to let well enough alone; and his rigid interpretation of the law, untempered by a sense of justice.

Gwynn Oak was owned by two brothers, James F. and David W. Price. It had been the target of periodic demonstrations by integrationists since 1952. The Price brothers nevertheless persisted in excluding Negroes from the park, maintaining that their white customers would not tolerate integration and that it would put the park out of business. Those Negroes who did manage to slip through the gates were verbally abused by park police and white patrons, ejected, arrested and, on several occasions, beaten. Demonstrators were charged with trespassing. They were invariably convicted and the convictions upheld by the state Court of Appeals, for, although Maryland had a public accommodations law, it did not apply to privately owned parks such as Gwynn Oak.

By 1963, however, the winds of change were sweeping across the country. Martin Luther King was planning his massive march on Washington, and Congress was debating the legislation that would eventually be passed as the historic Civil Rights Act of 1964. At Gwynn Oak two small but well-planned demonstrations had been carried out in May of that year, leading to the arrest, for trespassing, of a number of the demonstrators. In June, the Maryland Commission on Interracial Problems and Human Relations had invited the Price brothers to meet with them to discuss park admissions policy; when the brothers declined, they were informed by a commission spokesman that the integrationists would have no alternative but to demonstrate.

The answer to the Price brothers intransigence came in the form of the July 4th demonstration, which drew impressive support from across the country. Civil rights activists came from many states to seek arrest on the expected trespassing charges. For the first time at Gwynn Oak, white demonstrators outnumbered blacks. Also for the first time, Catholic clergymen from Baltimore participated in an actual demonstration; Monseigneur Austin J. Healy, a representative of the archdiocese of Baltimore, had specific diocesian permission to seek arrest. Other clergymen of high rank or national prominence included the Reverend Eugene Carson Blake, executive officer of the United Presbyterian Church in the United States; Bishop Daniel Corrigan of the National Council of Protestant Episcopal Churches; the Reverend Jon Regier of the National Council of Churches Emergency Commission on Religion and Race. The Reverend William Sloan Coffin, who was later to figure even more prominently in the movement against the war in Vietnam, was among those arrested, as was young Michael Schwerner, one of the three civil rights workers murdered in Philadelphia, Mississippi, less than a year later.

The International Ladies' Garment Workers' Union sent seven of its most experienced picket organizers to assist in keeping order. In integrated groups of ten to fifty, the demonstrators entered the park, where police made 275 arrests. The charge was trespassing; if a demonstrator went limp instead of walking to the school buses being used as paddy wagons, he was additionally charged with disorderly conduct. Only 100 went free on bail; the rest—175, including many of the clergymen—elected to remain in jail overnight.

James Price, shaken by the scope of the event, felt compelled to explain publicly that he had ordered the arrest of the clergymen, "the most difficult thing I have ever had to do. We felt we could not show less courage than the men of the cloth. Without attempting to debate the philosophic theories involved, we took the practical, sound businessman's approach to meeting the conditions of the world around us as we find them to be, and not perhaps as we would like them to be."

The demonstration had achieved its goal. A crisis now existed, and the community could no longer ignore the problem of Gwynn Oak. County Executive Agnew responded by calling for the immediate implementation, as an emergency measure, of a human relations commission created in a bill that was awaiting final action by the county council. If the commission proved unable to mediate the park issue, Agnew said he would add to its strength by empowering it both to hold hearings on complaints of segregation and to seek court injunctions in cases where illegal segregation was uncovered.

The commission had first been suggested to Agnew in March by Eugene L. King, Sr., a teacher in the public school system and an even-tempered, firm leader in the black community. Agnew's initial response was friendly but noncommittal. He said that he would need to have evidence of public support for such an agency. Two weeks later, King provided Agnew with evidence of white liberal support. At the same time he presented Agnew with a list of grievances from the black community, including the lack of suitable housing, the small number of Negro police and public school teachers in the county, discrimination in hiring and promotion policies in private industry and business, and the fact that Negroes were ignored in selecting members of county commissions and policy-making boards. Taking these grievances under advisement, Agnew asked for a list of specific tasks that the commission would perform. This too was provided, and Agnew requested the county council to create the commission.

The commission was something the integrationists and the

Negro community clearly wanted, but Agnew's announcement of its implementation at this particular moment must have seemed primarily designed to slow the momentum of the demonstrations. At best it came across as a typical kind of crisis reaction by Maryland government—the formation of a commission to take up a long-standing problem exactly one day too late.

The demonstrators managed to maintain their momentum, however. A committee of local clergymen who had been jailed on July 4th called on all pastors to appeal to their congregations to support another park protest two days later. About three hundred persons demonstrated on July 7; one hundred were arrested. Thousands of jeering, hooting whites turned out to harass the picketers. One white woman demonstrator was struck in the face by a rock. A Negro woman employee of the park was beaten by a gang of white youths who broke into a woman's rest room to get at her. Rocks were thrown at the school bus—paddy wagons. "This is a vicious crowd," Chief Robert Lally of the county police said at one point. "One little spark could set them off."

Agnew, however, reacted differently, questioning the actions of the demonstrators rather than the hatred expressed by the jeering crowds of whites. He said that he sympathized with the goals of the demonstrators, but doubted the wisdom of their means to those ends.

"In their impatience and resentment against an individual property owner the demonstrators have lost sight of . . . [their] reciprocal responsibilities. They have thrown, through hasty and immature decision, an undeserved burden upon the Baltimore County police force, which is sworn to uphold existing law.

"They have, without benefit, and probably with great harm to the high moral purpose of their movement, wasted the money of the taxpayers of Baltimore County. Regrettably, fairness and restraint have lost out to ill-advised haste and emotional self-hypnosis."

Agnew's remarks, which seem to waver between self-restraint and the abrasive language he has come to be noted for, were ignored by the demonstrators, perhaps because so many of them were in jail. At any rate, the remarks were irrelevant. A change was on its way, and county councils, police officials, judges and owners of places of public accommodation would have to accept it sooner or later.

Agnew now made an attempt to control the situation, meeting separately with the Price brothers and the integrationists. CORE (the Congress of Racial Equality), speaking for the movement, rejected Agnew's single suggestion that demonstrations be postponed into the coming weekend while an effort was made to reach an agreement. "Morally, I feel that the park should be integrated," Agnew volunteered. But then, pointing out that the state public accommodations law did not apply to the park, he said, ". . . the county is handcuffed. The Supreme Court or the state legislature must act." For a man as proud as Agnew, one who throughout his career has found it difficult to let others take the credit or tell him what to do, this is a curious admission of his own irrelevancy. It could be interpreted as an attempt to hide behind the law. The same expression of helplessness was to be repeated, with some variations, in response to other civil rights crises during his subsequent career. At any rate, in this instance he could not see any way to assist the demonstrators in their attempt to bring about a change that he claimed to accept as "morally" right. The demonstrators, however, were not perturbed. They announced more direct action.

On July 11, the newly created Baltimore County Human Relations Commission held a first organizational meeting. Michael G. Holofcener was elected chairman; G. Gordon Power was named vice chairman; and Eugene L. King, Sr., the Negro who had urged the commission's formation, was named secretary. The commission then announced its intentions of mediating the park dispute. On the following day, to establish a position from which negotiations could begin, it called on the integrationists to halt all demonstrations immediately and urged the park owners to integrate the park by July 26. As a show of good faith, the integrationists agreed to cease their activities. But for their part, the Price brothers rejected the suggestion to integrate. A second commission proposal that the park integrate the following spring was agreed to by the brothers on July 15, but the proposal was unacceptable to the integrationists.

This rejection wiped all proposals from the table. However,

in the four days of its existence the commission had accomplished a great deal toward reaching an area of accommodation: the demonstrations, even though they hung over the community as a continued threat, had been stopped for a time; the Price brothers at least had conceded that they were willing to integrate eventually; and the integrationists remained willing to settle for the July 26 date. Since the park normally closed early in September, except for a few additional weekends, only about five weeks of regular season days separated the two parties.

At this point Agnew, who had said he would remain aloof from the commission's mediating attempts, injected himself into the negotiations. He strongly urged the integrationists to accede to the lowering of the park's racial bars the following spring. Agnew's public statement said, "Although I have remained apart from actual negotiations in the matter, I feel that my official responsibility obliges me to urge acceptance of the settlement proposal." He had obviously found his voice and his sense of self-importance once again. He added that the spring integration would be "clearly a substantial victory for civil rights in this area."

The civil rights advocates were incensed, as were members of the human relations commission. Agnew seemed to be imposing his will in the matter and, to the integrationists, it looked like an attempt to shift the settlement away from the commission Agnew had appointed to "the court of public opinion." The long wait until spring would not be acceptable to the mass of demonstrators, the leaders believed. Furthermore, the Price brothers already had suggested that the spring integration effort be reviewed after thirty days in case the "social experiment" prove to be chaotic "as we believe it may be." This could mean that any trouble fomented by segregationists could bring the situation right back to where it now was. Furthermore, G. Gordon Power, the commission vice chairman, had spelled out a danger in the proposal: since it would seem a reasonable one to most of the community, it was likely to increase the resentment against further demonstrations. Agnew's support of the proposal clearly increased the likelihood of this reaction, further reducing the integrationists' area for maneuvering.

Holofcener, the commission chairman, issued a strong statement censuring Agnew. In the first place, Agnew was urging
the acceptance of a proposal that was already dead. The commission itself had been no more committed to the spring 1964
date than it had been to the July 26, 1963, date. Both had been
put forward as negotiating points to be used to work toward
some acceptable middle ground. Now Agnew had made a
power play on one side. Holofcener said any public statements
by the county executive or any other official would be "prejudicial" to the mediation efforts. "Considering the delicate
nature of the discussions and the high feelings on both sides,
we fail to see any useful purpose in such pronouncements,"
Holofcener said. "In fact, because of the possibility of misunderstanding more harm than good is likely." It was a severe
rebuke, and one that Agnew would not forget.

Meanwhile, although the Ad Hoc Committee to Desegregate
Gwynn Oak held to its agreement to stay all demonstrations,
two of the demonstrators quickly formed a new group, "Operation Manpower," and announced their group would mobilize
new demonstrations on the coming weekend. The following
day, the Maryland Council of Churches, an agency of more
than two thousand Protestant and Orthodox churches, endorsed nonviolent demonstrations and called on member
churches to support racial desegregation efforts in the state.

Support for the weekend demonstrations built up into a
threat that would finally force the issue. Integrationist leaders
and the park owners met with the commission negotiators in
an eight-hour session ending at 4 A.M. The Price brothers
offered to integrate on September 1, just before the close of
the regular season. The integrationists rejected this token proposal, but offered to accept an August 26 date. Six days now
separated each side. The police department was notified by the
integrationists that demonstrations would resume the following day. Police Chief Lally was told to expect 300 picketers.
A workshop on nonviolent techniques was hastily set up for
that evening. Holofcener gloomily prophesized, "We face
nothing but bloodshed."

Agnew now interceded once more, and this time with great
effect. Throughout the day he negotiated by telephone with
both sides. Then, at a hastily called night meeting at the

county office building, Agnew, the park owners, the integration leaders and several of the human relations commission members patched together an agreement. A compromise date of August 28 was accepted. The Price brothers agreed to inform the state's attorney that they preferred to have all charges dropped against 383 white and Negro demonstrators who had been arrested. Groups of clergymen offered to help promote new business at the area. Twelve hours before another non-violent assault was to begin, the demonstrations were called off.

A harried James Price, convinced he faced financial ruin, was resigned rather than rancorous. "It's just hard to fight when the archbishop and the leaders of the Protestant faiths and the Jewish faith, and let's face it, the President and the governor and other governmental leaders tell you what should be, plus the union leaders—to say nothing of a nudging here and there from CORE and the NAACP."

On August 28, as 200,000 whites and blacks peacefully gathered at the Lincoln Memorial in Washington to hear Martin Luther King intone "I have a dream . . . ," Sharon Langley, a black eleven-month-old baby with her thumb stuck firmly in her mouth, was lifted by her father onto a spotted horse on the merry-go-round at Gwynn Oak Amusement Park. Two small white boys climbed on animals on either side of her. It was the first integrated amusement at the park. Neither the Langleys nor the small white boys or their mother had taken part in the demonstrations or were connected with any of the integration organizations as far as the press could determine. Nearly all the integrationist leaders and their followers were at the Washington march. In October 1964, a year and a half after the breakthrough, Agnew signed a public accommodations law into effect, and the state's attorney, who had obstinately refused to drop the 730 cases against Gwynn Oak Park demonstrators, declared the cases "moot" and wiped them off the books. The park is still operating; business is still good.

Agnew's role in the integration of the park was to loom larger in the minds of segregationists than integrationists. He had publicly endorsed integration as "morally" right, a considerable concession for many public officials in Maryland at the time, and he had, finally, helped hammer out the settlement. But to tireless, hard-working integrationists such as the Reverend Marion Bascomb, Agnew could have done no less, in view of the new attitudes sweeping the nation and the powerful support and momentum of the demonstrations in the county. Furthermore, it had been necessary to push him as hard as the Price brothers, who never claimed they were morally opposed to segregation.

It is apparent in retrospect that every interim position of the county executive favored a delay in integration, a cessation of the demonstrations that were finally to prove so effective, and official encouragement of public opinion against the demonstrators. He had, furthermore, weakened the credibility of his "moral" support of integration, by arguing at one point that the increased costs of law enforcement resulting from the demonstrations were of greater community concern than the goal of the protests. On balance, to Mr. Bascomb, Agnew could be given no higher mark than any other public official unwilling to endure a disruption of public order in his constituency for the sake of social justice. The judgment might have been harsher had anyone pointed out at the time that James Price had been one of Agnew's early financial supporters in the 1962 campaign, a fact, if made known, which would have placed in serious question Agnew's professed position as an impartial mediator.

One small, unpublicized incident speaks a great deal for the patience of the civil rights leadership and their dedication to their goals in the face of personal dangers, injuries and insults. At one meeting, when the situation was particularly tense, Agnew opened the conversation by looking directly at the Reverend Mr. Bascomb and saying, "Every time I see you I am repulsed." Mr. Bascomb chose not to exploit the statement publicly, but it fixed in his mind an estimation of this public official whom he would have to confront again and again in the next few years. Regardless of how high Agnew's political climb might take him, it was the man revealed by that statement that Mr. Bascomb would regard as the true Agnew.

6 GWYNN OAK WAS the major civil rights victory in the area, but it was only one thrust in a scattered attack on segregated public accommodations. From the Gwynn Oak confrontation, integrationists got not only good experience but also new cohorts for direct action against other types of recreational facilities, particularly privately owned community swimming pools and roller rinks. Demonstrations against these segregated facilities increased in August and September. Agnew's public statements in connection with such demonstrations gave him the reputation of being a civil rights liberal and an integrationist, particularly in the eyes of those strongly opposed to integration, but also among more moderate whites in the community. When a county magistrate failed to hold a proper hearing for two roller rink demonstrators, refused to release them on bail and, over their lawyers' objections, ordered them committed for mental examinations, Agnew made vehement public objection. His efforts to see that anti-discrimination clauses were inserted into contracts let by the county to private firms added to his liberal reputation. In October 1963, he received the "Helping Hand" award from the Metropolitan Civic Association for appointing the Human Relations Commission. An even surer sign that he was regarded as a liberal came in January 1964: a scurrilous handbill distributed by the Maryland chapter of the national States' Rights party linked him, along with Negro leaders, to known communists.

Civil rights activists, however, found him to be inconsistent and unpredictable. They were particularly irritated by his tendency to attack them for causing public disruption rather than segregationists for thwarting the progress of the integration he claimed to believe in. In September 1963, for instance,

44

while urging that charges against the Gwynn Oak demonstrators be dropped, he maintained in the same statement that the swimming pool demonstrations then being held "served no useful purpose except to overburden the county." He appeared to favor integration, but to oppose integrationists; to oppose segregation, yet to show a great deal of sympathy for segregationists.

Agnew did accept "peaceful" picketing as appropriate protest. But a "peaceful" protest meant to him a limited number of demonstrators, and no direct action such as encouraging arrests by trespassing onto segregated facilities. It was understandable to civil rights leaders like Walter Carter of CORE that an administrative official would be upset, annoyed, even angered, by techniques involving large and volatile gatherings of people, mass arrests and crowded court dockets. But, on the other hand, if Agnew were as sympathetic to their goals as he professed to be, he should have been able to understand in return that such nonviolent but disruptive tactics were the only real teeth the civil rights movement had.

Agnew's early relationship with the Human Relations Commission he had created did nothing to increase his standing with the integrationists. Throughout Maryland at that time such commissions more often than not were restricted to a rigidly impartial role, unable to act except on evidence that the law was being violated, which was precisely the kind of role County Executive Agnew felt they ought to play. They were not to be instruments of change, nor actual advocates of integration; in fact their membership was often composed of segregationists. The Baltimore County commission, however, had in its chairman, Mr. Holofcener, a vigorous advocate of the integrationist cause. He was too vigorous for Agnew, who in November 1963 called for Holofcener's resignation. But the eleven-member commission itself did not join in Agnew's call, and the chairman refused to resign.

In a statement to the commission, Agnew clarified his position and renewed his personal opposition to the chairman. "The Negro is entitled as a matter of moral right to have his civil equality legislated and enforced," Agnew said, but he insisted on a need for "a diminuation of the aggressive posture favoring racial integration reflected by the chairman of this commission." As seemed to be the case whenever Agnew addressed himself to the question of civil rights, this statement is clouded by ambiguity; in fact, it very nearly contradicts itself.

In all such feuds between public figures, it is difficult to be certain which of several possible contributing factors should be given most weight. Agnew's attempt to purge Holofcener may not have been determined as much by political considerations as by personal dislike and vindictiveness; some sort of retaliation for Holofcener's public rebuke of Agnew during the Gwynn Oak affair was long overdue. Another factor that could have affected Agnew's decision was his pride of office; it might well have seemed to him that the kind of initiative shown by Holofcener trespassed upon the perquisites of the county executive.

But whichever of these factors most influenced Agnew, it soon became clear even to Holofcener's strongest supporters that the feud could serve only to cripple the commission's future effectiveness. Despite their misgivings as to whom Agnew might appoint to replace him, his friends urged him to resign as chairman, which he did near the end of the year. The following June, when Holofcener's term expired, Agnew refused to reappoint him even as a member of the commission. Holofcener went out, accusing Agnew of "vacillating with the winds of political expediency" and of "trying to be all things to all men." Agnew, however, replaced Holofcener with a chairman suggested by Holofcener's supporters, one who would not substantially alter the controlling balance of the commission.

A week after Holofcener resigned as chairman, Agnew told the commission, "Despite charges to the contrary from some areas, I do not want a soft, do-nothing policy." He promised "the full weight" of his administration behind the commission's two clear targets: "To overcome through whatever means are necessary the discriminatory practices that deprive Negroes of their public rights" and "to provide a better climate for voluntary social acceptance of the Negro through sensitive persuasion not militant pushing." He could be taken at his words; his actions in the ensuing year would support them. But his language, in phrases such as "militant pushing," continued to hold civil rights advocates up to scorn.

In August 1964, Agnew fulfilled a promise to CORE

leaders by submitting an administration civil rights bill covering several major areas of complaint—swimming pools, roller rinks, amusement parks and employment opportunities—but excluding real estate transactions and other housing provisions. In keeping with his promise, he urged the county council to consider the bill immediately, although it finally decided to withhold action until after the elections in November.

His involvement with another issue played a major part in establishing his early reputation as a "liberal" and an outspoken proponent of Negro efforts to integrate the nation. The previous Democratic administration had fostered a plan for an urban renewal program in the county, and it had been supported by the voters in a referendum in 1960. Agnew endorsed the program in 1963, but by this time conservative opposition to it had been mobilized; it was labeled a socialistic, even communistic scheme. It was said to attack the rights of personal property and to have as its unstated goal the integration of private dwelling places.

Actually, the plan was directed at industrial development and did not include any provisions for public housing or the resettlement of populations. Furthermore, only one small Negro residential area was affected by the plan and it would have been of little benefit to the Negro community. Nevertheless, reports concerning other urban renewal programs and the problems they had caused in other parts of the nation were problems publicized in Baltimore County; the program was soundly defeated in a second referendum. It was not an issue which actually concerned Negroes or civil rights, but Agnew's opponents implied or said that it did, and the charges assumed a truth of their own. Once more Agnew, who had supported the plan because of its economic benefits, was pictured as a racial liberal without having earned the designation. In the short run, it was to hurt him severely with the conservative white community. In the long run, it was to help elect him governor.

Agnew neither learned nor changed because of his experience with civil rights issues in the county. The effect on him was to harden positions he had held before having to deal with the issues from the administrative seat of government. He held to his lawyerly concern for community order and for due process. His concern for community order worked against the integrationists; his concern for due process sometimes worked against them, sometimes for them. Demonstrations cost the community money and disrupted its normal routine; the fact that they were the only possible way to achieve goals which he claimed to support in no way impressed him as a justification. The due process of the courts, Agnew held, was the only legitimate way to achieve progress in integration, however slow it might be. Yet once a man had been arrested, Agnew did insist that he be treated fairly before the law. Bound by his positions, Agnew developed no trust, no respect and no understanding of black activists; actions he later took as governor would indicate, on the contrary, that he had developed strong personal antipathies for those black leaders who disregarded his advice or challenged his authority.

Agnew had seen hatred in the faces of white citizens stirred up by Negro demands, had witnessed the cold determination of black and white nonviolent demonstrators. He had not liked the experience or the intense emotions that direct confrontations aroused. One day, his wife called him to say that pickets were marching in front of his house. She was frightened and when Agnew reached home, he became frightened also. The problems of the Negroes properly belonged in his office. Now they had been "brought home" to him. It was an affront to him and a threat to his family. More than anything else this was to crystallize his distaste for demonstrators, for those who chose to become disturbers of the peace in the fight for their cause. These experiences did not move him from his repeated position that segregation was "morally" wrong and ought to be eliminated from American life. Yet he seemed always to reserve his most penetrating invective for the integrationists.

On December 9, 1963, Agnew gave a statement on civil rights to the Baltimore County Human Relations Commission. It illuminates many aspects of his attitude toward the achievement of an integrated society. His belief in such a society is repeated, but he maintains that "social acceptance" cannot be legislated, because it depends on the individual's "voluntary acceptance by one man of another as a companion." He decries the "hatreds of segregationist dogma," but does not have a word to say against the segregationist as a man. Personal vilification is reserved for civil rights activists, who are described as "malcontent opportunists," "chauvinistic self-seekers" and "fair-weather friends."

Agnew has often been pictured as a civil rights moderate or even liberal who, following the Baltimore riots of 1968, turned into a conservative overnight. In fact, his position has always been the same. The circumstances in which that position has been held have, however, continually changed; and it is the shifting circumstances that have created the illusion of a change in substance. For this reason, the December 1963 statement, which follows below, makes very illuminating reading.

The greatest enemies of effective, intelligent government are opportunists who have learned that a measure of popularity can be cheaply purchased by boldly assuming oversimplified positions on highly complex, volatile issues. But the real danger lies not with these chauvinistic self-seekers, whose insincerity is sooner or later detected, but with their well-motivated but poorly informed sympathizers.

These average citizens, mentally fatigued after a day in the arena of private enterprise, are quick to seize upon the simple, clearly defined opinion and all too often prefer it to the enlightened viewpoint that focuses strongly in those troublesome gray areas of doubt. It is difficult to criticize the average citizen for not having the energy to become expert in fields not related to his vocation.

So, unfortunately, many turn to the oversimplified demi-truths of the lunatic fringes of any emotional dispute. They proudly identify themselves as "liberals" or "conservatives," take predetermined stances on matters about which they have insufficient knowledge and, when controversial issues arise, generally make it extremely difficult for those in positions of governmental responsibility.

Not since the early and bloody days of the labor movement has there been more fertile soil for the malcontent opportunists than the hatreds of segregationist dogma on the one hand and the unreasonable ultimatums of some power-crazed integrationist leaders on the other.

Caught up in the searing heat of deprivation by the

decade, the Negro is eager to have civil equality legislated and enforced. This he is entitled to as a moral right if our system of government and our way of life is to have meaning. I repeat, so that I may never again be misunderstood, the Negro is entitled as a matter of moral right to have his civil equality legislated and enforced. . . .

Open occupancy legislation, the attempted crashing of private membership clubs, unlawful trespassing and unlawful demonstrating, violate the civil rights of the Negro. Social acceptance can never be legislated because it is the voluntary acceptance by one man of another as a companion, not the acceptance by one race of another in casual contact.

I take a strong position that it is wrong to tell the owner of a private dwelling place, be it single family or multiple unit, that he must offer it for rent or sale to anyone with whom he does not wish to do business. This applies whether or not he is biased and applies regardless of what his bias may embrace. If he dislikes Greeks, he should not have to deal with Greeks, and the government that infringes upon his discretion in this respect abrogates his freedom of selection and disregards the intent of the Constitution of the United States.

On the other hand, when an individual openly or impliedly seeks the good will and business of the general public, I believe he thereby waives his rights to personal preference. He then becomes obligated to sell his product or render his services to all persons who present themselves as prospective customers, so long as they do not by their conduct or demeanor offend his other clientele. . . .

We have undertaken an arduous and difficult task. Patience is a word that has apparently lost most of its meaning in the rush to right the wrongs that have been done our Negro citizens for so many years. Yet patience is an absolute necessity if these wounds are to heal properly from the inside out and not become deep-lying and festering infections under superficial mending.

The fact that the Negro lacks confidence in those who select the surer but less sensational path is not surprising. He looks at a history of unfulfilled promises while he is concurrently being goaded by those same self-seeking opportunists who constantly demand the sensational. When the rash conduct of others makes his position untenable, these same fair-weather friends depart for distant geographic points and leave the local Negro holding the bag.

It is an obligation of this Human Relations Commission to protect our Negro community against exploitation by politically motivated opportunists and to see that steady progress, rather than the "jump forward two, slip back three" type is implemented.

As the chief elected official of this county I have been attacked by those who call me a pawn of the integration movement, but I have been attacked no less strongly by those who vilify me as an ardent segregationist. I state to you with sincerity that the words of this statement accurately reflect my conviction on this subject. They are offered without fear for the purpose of clarification and to make a clear permanent record.

7

HARDLY HAD Richard M. Nixon announced his vice-presidential running mate in 1968 than the black civil rights leadership in Maryland, shocked by the selection, announced a nationwide campaign aimed at his defeat.

These were the very same black leaders who had organized two years before to ensure Angew's election as governor. But that was in 1966, when they had chosen Spiro T. Agnew to steer the state away from a threatening white backlash. That was the year Americans for Democratic Action endorsed Agnew for governor. That was the year Agnew fought against a surprisingly strong rally of conservative and ultra-right elements in Maryland.

Actually, Agnew the Liberal never existed. He had to be invented, and he was, in two stages. The first stage involved the issue of urban renewal in Baltimore County. The second stage developed during the race for governor.

Agnew had tied himself so closely to urban renewal, argued so personally for it, that the defeat, when it came, included him. He had been unable to extricate himself from the issue before the referendum and was unable to separate himself from the defeat. Therefore he made three attempts to revive urban renewal in an altered form. Each time he was defeated by the county council; each time he further alienated large segments of the voting public. Finally, when the county's delegation to the state General Assembly got through a state bill abolishing the county's rehabilitation and renewal commission, Agnew appealed to the governor to veto the bill. The governor refused and the issue of urban renewal was dead. But Agnew was not known as a liberal.

Agnew was fatally wounded in the county by the liberal label—in much the same way that he himself would shoot down senatorial candidates as "radical-liberals" in the 1970 off-year elections. Agnew did not deserve the label; no liberal would have recognized the kinship. Nevertheless, the word alone did the trick; Agnew acknowledged to himself that he could not win a second term as county executive. Briefly, he investigated the possibilities of attaining a judgeship, this time by appointment, but that alternative continued to remain closed to him and he began to look to the governor's race as his best chance of moving upward in politics. As the highest Republican officeholder in the state, the gubernatorial nomination was a solid possibility.

Agnew had not been an active party member or shown interest in party affairs beyond the needs of his own ambitious ventures. He had done little to build the party in the county and had paid scant attention to the state party organization; most of the party leaders did not know him. J. Glenn Beall, now U.S. Senator from Maryland, was minority leader in the Maryland House of Delegates while Agnew was county executive. He does not recall ever having seen Agnew at a state party function during the first two and a half years of his term. Nevertheless, Agnew set about winning encouragement for the gubernatorial race.

In September 1965, Agnew joined other elected Republicans in a state meeting on party strategy. Beall was there, as were Congressmen Charles Mathias (now U.S. Senator) and Rogers Morton (later named by Nixon to head the national GOP party organization and then appointed Secretary of the Interior). Agnew left the meeting assured that he would have the unanimous endorsement of the party leaders if he decided to enter the gubernatorial race. That blessing was available from the top, but Agnew had a very real problem in letting the rest of the party know of his existence. He began a series of speaking engagements throughout the state, particularly in the bedroom counties near the District of Columbia. His talks gave him some satisfying headlines and stirred the interest of the rank and file. Democrats were "liars, vote buyers, stiflers of initiative and intruders into private, local areas of life," he said in a typical speech.

For the first five months of 1966, Agnew concentrated on rallying the party to his support. He took advantage of every opportunity for radio and television coverage in Baltimore and Washington, garnering the valuable free time that would no longer be available once he formally announced his candidacy.

In January, a booster gave a cocktail party for Agnew and the press. In February, Agnew tentatively engaged the Baltimore advertising firm of I. Robert Goodman to plan his media campaign. He hired a still photographer, R. R. Rodney Boyce, to compile a file of photographs for later publicity purposes, and a public relations staff to help him build an image and identification around the state. Some of his aides were sent to New York City and to Harrisburg, Pennsylvania, to get campaign tips from the staffs of Mayor John Lindsay and Governor William Scranton. He developed position papers and started issuing them. And he hired Cynthia Rosenwald, a young Baltimore housewife and mother, as a research assistant and occasional speech writer. (Mrs. Rosenwald so completely captured the essential Agnew, his thought processes and speech patterns, that she remained with him for nearly four years, through his years as governor, the 1968 presidential campaign, and into his first year as Vice President, with its joltingly memorable early speeches.)

Agnew managed to enlist Tilton H. Dobbin, president of the Maryland National Bank, as his campaign treasurer. One of the bank's assistant vice presidents became the campaign bookkeeper and comptroller. Clarke Langrall, a Baltimore County insurance executive, was the principal staff fund raiser. Agnew also organized a finance committee of wealthy businessmen and industrialists from the Baltimore area. Most of his financial advisers were Democrats and his campaign funds came mostly from Democrats; in heavily Democratic Maryland a Republican had to look to these sources. Meanwhile, the publicity campaign continued. By spring, the Democratic contenders were surfacing and the looming fight within that party began squeezing Agnew's uncontested primary bid into the lesser columns of the newspapers.

On April 17, with all these initial preparations out of the way, Agnew announced his official entry in the race. The statement itself, having undergone much fussing and rewriting, promised "a unified forthright program dealing with all aspects of our state and its people." "I have learned," said Agnew the county executive, "that the problems which face our people . . . are real and . . . demand real answers." He had "a firm conviction that dynamic leadership will allow Maryland to face the challenges of a modern society in a modern way." Copies of the speech were available to every news medium accompanied by an "official" biography and photograph; recordings were available for the radio stations; taping appointments were kept at the metropolitan television studios. Three days later, Agnew filed his candidacy with the Maryland Secretary of State as the law required, and Republican officeholders and party officials gathered enthusiastically about him to show how excited they were over his candidacy. The reporters and cameras dutifully recorded it all. Politeness and fair play on the part of the media, not professional judgment, made Agnew's busywork into medium-big news. Professional judgment would come into full focus when the Democratic party's big league opened its season.

No one could foresee the direction of the 1966 gubernatorial campaign when Agnew decided to become a candidate. The possibility of Agnew's victory certainly was not discernible. The ratio of Democrats to Republicans in the state in 1966 was 3½ to 1. There was no lack of candidates who could make a strong bid on the Democratic side. A tough, wide-open primary fight was looming for the Democrats, that was certain. But in previous years, as recently as 1962, intra-party fighting had not been lastingly harmful; it had served to invigorate the Democrats for the general elections.

There were two serious Democratic primary candidates, Thomas J. Finan and Carleton Sickles; a third entrant, George Mahoney, was given no conceivable odds of winning.

Thomas J. Finan, the Attorney General, was the nose-clean party man. He had given the Democrats loyalty and hard work for some time; the party, in turn, had prepared to have him as a Maryland governor. He was the organization's man, the man for the Baltimore City Democratic machine and for the machines of the counties. He was the heir-apparent to the incumbent governor, Millard J. Tawes, and in a normal, uneventful year, the nomination and the office would have passed to him.

In the jargon of political labelers, Finan was a moderate, but he is better described as a supporter of the status quo—although not exactly a rock in that respect either. He could, without difficulty, receive and accept all the personal and financial support that the pary and the administration commanded. He was lackluster, but this was of no consequence. His biggest liability was imbedded in the source of his support. The Tawes administration was coming to an end amid rankling dissatisfaction on several issues of statewide interest, particularly a tax reform proposal that was bogged down by narrow, regional thinking, and a proposal for a new bridge across Chesapeake Bay that, to many people, seemed to smell of ulterior motives, financial favoritism and possibly corruption. Finan was of that administration; there would be no way he could lay down the burden of its record when he ran on his own. On balance, however, the support of the party organization weighed more heavily than the record of the administration. He was the favorite.

The principal challenger was Carleton Sickles, then serving his second term as congressman-at-large. He was a liberal with credentials to prove it—an ultra-liberal, according to Maryland's political lexicon. Sickles was confident enough of his chances to give up his congressional seat in order to make the race. He expected to draw heavily in the Washington, D.C., suburban counties of Montgomery and Prince Georges and among liberals and blacks in Baltimore City. He would have no standing in Maryland's Eastern Shore region, which is Deep South compared to the rest of the state. In a general election, Sickles would have to rely on the Democratic organization and strong labor support in blue collar areas, but he expected to make inroads into normal Republican support.

Most observers believed that Sickles was isolated too far to the left to capture the nomination in a two-way primary race. Finan, stolidly in the middle, would have captured all of the votes he was sitting on and everything in sight to his right. However, the third candidate, George Mahoney, offered Sickles a chance. Clearly, Mahoney would attract none of Sickles' votes; possibly he would take enough away from Finan to give Sickles the election.

George Mahoney, by 1966, had become the elder statesman

of the also-rans. Over the years he had entered so many state-wide races that newsmen did not bother to count them any more. He was sixty-four years old. He had risen from day laborer to successful paving contractor. He had a substantial personal fortune, custom-made suits, and a young, blonde, extremely attractive wife who campaigned with him. Continually, he told the state that so many people had urged him to run for office that he felt it a duty to oblige, and although he never won an election, he always gathered about 100,000 votes.

As a speaker, whether on television or before a live audience, Mahoney was so bad as to be indescribable. People said he was illiterate and simply could not read the speeches that were written for him; that perhaps his eyesight was so poor he couldn't discern the type; or that he must certainly have been drunk when they saw him. Even his good friends suffered through his performances. But Mahoney was an amiable, soft-spoken, mannerly, even courtly man. People liked him and he inevitably found those 100,000 voters to support him. To newspaper editors and others who looked somberly on the game of politics, Mahoney was an annoyance and a bore. But he always had to be figured in, not as a winner, but as an element that might upset the other candidates.

The Agnew staff hoped that Sickles would win. They could visualize a campaign against him, allowing Agnew to run an ideological campaign placing himself somewhat to the left of center and being the logical choice of everyone except the few voters attracted to an "ultra-liberal." Finan would be harder to fight. The Democratic organization would be undivided and strong in his support. It would be more difficult to gather the Democratic crossover votes that Agnew needed for a victory. Sickles would give the Agnew forces something to chew on. Finan was like cotton candy, and without coloring, even at that. He was a physically attractive, neartly dressed man with no discernible philosophic markings. He was, in fact, a short version of Spiro Agnew and, given the Democratic party's registered strength, the similarity was bound to prove a drawback to Agnew.

The image of Agnew as rather tall and Finan as rather short seems to have struck the fancy of Agnew's tentatively employed advertising firm, I. Robert Goodman. The strongest theme they could come up with was the slogan "He Stands Tall." The idea was vetoed. Even Agnew's staff was appalled at this attempt to make physical stature stand in for political stature. Eventually the image-makers centered their efforts around a song, "Ted Agnew's My Kind of Man" without being too specific about what kind of man that was.

The important image-making was not to be bought, however. It came for free in the character of George Mahoney's campaign. Although Mahoney started out with a self-defeating slogan touched with humor, "Yes—Again!" midway through the primaries his campaign took another form, became deadly serious and eventually dictated the course of the election.

Two years before, in 1964, Alabama's George Wallace had entered the presidential primary in Maryland and had captured four of every ten Democratic votes that were cast. It was a surprising and dismaying showing to the racial moderates in the state who had rallied strongly in an effort to beat him decisively. Now, in 1966, with Sickles entrenched among the liberals and Attorney General Finan sprawled in the pragmatic, undefinable political middle, Mahoney was advised to stake his claim on the right. He did so, building his entire effort around one issue—opposition to open housing laws. Mahoney's slogan was inspired and powerful: "Your home is your castle—Protect It." It conjured up images of onslaughts of racial integrationists, demonstrators, socialists invading rights of property, to say nothing of burglars, armed robbers and rapists. Mahoney's campaign caught fire. Those citizens who were not enlisted in his cause were stirred by the disquieting memories of Wallace's unexpected showing two years before.

Agnew's camp had not wasted any time considering the possibility of a Mahoney victory. But as the campaign extended into August, that likelihood began to seem less remote. Accordingly, Agnew's campaign began a slight shift to the left, seeking the most promising position from which to combat Mahoney. Agnew began to give some attention to civil rights questions, a development that in some cases required careful engineering. For instance, in endorsing the federal anti-poverty program, he had to overcome public statements made four months before, when he had denounced the program as "a dangerous invasion of our constitutional rights." He had seen no need for an anti-poverty agency in Baltimore County "whatsoever." But that was in March, before he had announced his candidacy, and now it was July and Mahoney clearly was preempting all of the votes likely to be attracted by such statements. Agnew lamely explained that he had feared a lack of governmental supervision. A program responsive to elected officials was something else, however. "I have supported the establishment of such a program . . . from the time it was first recommended," he said. Although he had consistently opposed local legislation for open occupancy in private housing, he now agreed to support limited statewide open occupancy legislation if he became governor. His plan would cover all new houses and commercial apartments but would exclude existing houses.

Agnew found it expedient to proclaim himself "the only candidate for governor with a record of solid achievement in civil right gains." And he defended not only his accomplishments but his motivation. "My positions on civil rights have not been evolved as a political end. After all, how many votes could I expect in a county with only three per cent Negro population?" His brief program for civil rights included such irrelevant, far-distant possibilities as planned cities in which haphazard growth would be replaced with carefully structured integrated communities. He spoke of enlarged educational and employment opportunities, but reserved his strongest statements for the "tool of moral persuasion." "Black Power in the finest sense will come from responsible Negro leadership and total community acceptance," he said.

The primaries took place on September 13. Mahoney won the Democratic flag, much to the dismay of white moderates who had come to believe that through slow, painful social progress the state had left behind the attitudes and prejudices that had made Wallace appealing. Wallace had exposed the racialism that the blacks in the state knew all along to be present. Now George Mahoney was working the same vein with fearful ramifications. Mahoney followers, other conservatives, and the state's segregationist element were elated; the rest of the state was thrown into panic. The Democratic nomination was tantamount to election. It was only a question of whether the party would accept into its fold the maverick who had already sneaked off with the nomination.

A statewide research staff put together by Agnew had compiled data to be used in a post-primary effort calling for the support of Democrats whose own candidates were defeated in the primary and who might be lured to Agnew's side for the general election. There were dossiers on key individuals who might be enlisted into active roles on Agnew's behalf; and there were plans for volunteer organizations for disgruntled Democrats. As soon as the primary results were in, calls went out from Agnew headquarters to staff aides of the two defeated Democrats, inviting them to assist in the Agnew campaign. Mahoney's victory made this raiding more successful than had been anticipated. The Democratic party was in disarray; its leadership was reluctant to support Mahoney and was faced with no realistic alternative. Individual Democrats agonized over their courses of action and many decided that turning to Agnew, or dropping out of sight, were the only acceptable choices.

The statistics of the primaries defined Agnew's task. There had been a total of 118,482 Republican votes. Agnew had received 98,000, the rest being scattered among several minor candidates. The Democratic total was 491,265. Mahoney had not received a majority, but his 148,000 votes were well above Agnew's total and more than the total Republican turnout. Mahoney had, in fact, gathered barely more than one out of every three Democratic votes and won by fewer than 1,900 votes over Sickles. Finan, the heir-apparent, had finished third with 134,216. For victory, Agnew needed to attract a substantial number of the 280,700 Democratic voters who had not been with Mahoney in the primary. He would have to rely heavily on the liberal vote from the population centers of Baltimore City and the Washington suburbs. In addition, the Negro vote of Baltimore City was going to be crucial. Most politicians believed that the Baltimore City black vote would have to be heavy and solidly for Agnew if he were to win.

Negroes comprise one-half of Baltimore City's total population of about 950,000. Elsewhere in the state, Negroes are a political cipher and, except for Cambridge on the Eastern Shore, had been quiescent in civil rights activities. Baltimore, as the state's only large city, contains the only real center for black civil rights activity and is the only major population center of significant political numbers. A few Negroes sit on the city council, a few are state representatives, and two were state senators. Negroes are now getting on the court benches and into important city offices, but these advances are quite recent and small indeed in terms of black potential strength.

The fact is that Baltimore Negroes have been extremely unsophisticated in politics and have yet to fully emerge as a political force. Their vote is corruptly controlled by "walk around money," a euphemism for the actual purchase of votes, precinct by precinct, at a standard price, which may be as little as a half pint of whiskey or as much as a few dollars. Under Maryland law it was always legal to pay for the services of election day workers to watch the polls for evidence of fraud, to hand out literature, to contact voters and to do other tasks. This practice, with its legal cover, easily operated as a simple vote-purchase. It was not unusual for the Democratic machine to have on their worker "payroll" every person voting for their candidate in a precinct. Controlling the Negro vote had only to do with spreading the money election day— and perhaps spreading a little around before the election to make certain there were no opposition offers to outbid on election day itself.

In return for their votes the Negroes got the whiskey or the two bucks and nothing else. What Negro politicians were concerned with, having been groomed in this kind of system, had little to do with civil rights, justice in the courts or mercy at the hands of the police. It was not civil rights groups that delivered the votes or civil rights issues that gathered them to a candidate. The votes were delivered by old-time black and white politicians in the Democratic (white) machine, and black numbers racketeers absorbed by the white-controlled rackets. The question in the 1966 campaign was whether or not black leaders could for the first time deliver the black vote.

The black leaders committed themselves to Agnew quickly. Public endorsements of Agnew from black politicians and civic leaders began pouring into his headquarters before primary night was over. Open housing may have been the overt subject of Mahoney's slogan, but the issue was race and if

Mahoney did not acknowledge this, the rest of the state saw it clearly. In that context it was not surprising that Agnew also received the personal endorsement of prominent Democratic liberals, even those of such esteem as Dean Acheson, the former Secretary of State, who saw in the Maryland election the threat of a reactionary white backlash that could loom into national significance. It was not even surprising, then (although it is almost unbelievable now) that Agnew received the endorsement of the Americans for Democratic Action (ADA).

The drive toward the general election had its own complicating elements. Hyman A. Pressman, Baltimore City comptroller and a Democrat, had engaged in a petition campaign and was on the ballot as an independent. Pressman is a Jewish leprechaun, a lawyer given to performing all kinds of legal tricks to frustrate the efforts of city hall, the courts, or the legislature when he feels that the interests of "the little man" are threatened. His victories in these causes had given him substantial support in the city and he continued to fight city hall even after joining it as comptroller. Pressman wrote funny but terrible poems in commemoration of everything and recited his doggerel in city council meetings, at public hearings and anywhere else in the city. A tiny, sprightly man, he marched in St. Patrick's Day parades, Columbus Day parades and whenever the spirit moved him, strutting along unabashedly by himself—no part of any other marching unit, but the same cocky, independent exhibitionist he was in politics.

But he had his following. The blue collar class liked him; he was gutsy, always ready to fight the public utilities or anybody else. He might also cut into the liberal bloc by winning sentimental support from the large Jewish vote. And he might carry well in some of the Negro wards. And so the probabilities of Pressman's presence added another uncertainty to the race. However, no one could do much about Pressman in any event. Mahoney and Agnew went about their campaigns concentrating on each other.

The victory of Mahoney brought an outpouring of support from around the state for Agnew; it was an intoxicating experience for the Republicans. The bulk of Agnew's campaign money had come from fund-raising dinners, businessmen's luncheons, personal appeals to wealthy individuals and other efforts of the state Republican committee. Now new Democratic coffers opened to Agnew and financial support from wealthy Montgomery County and Baltimore City turned from a trickle into a torrent. Agnew and his advisers began to feel that Mahoney would be a pushover. Instead of making a concentrated attack on Mahoney, Agnew was presenting himself as if his election were a mere formality. But this strategy changed when it became obvious from polls that Mahoney was striking an extremely responsive chord, and that Agnew was not making the inroads among Democratic voters that were necessary.

Mahoney was avoiding face-to-face confrontations, for the same reasons that Mike Birmingham had in the election for county executive four years earlier. Agnew was obviously the more attractive figure; Mahoney didn't want to give the voters the opportunity to make a direct comparison. He refused to debate Agnew on television, saying, "I am not running against [the other candidates] . . . I am running against things as they are."

On both sides, the campaign became more personal. In frustration, Agnew was characterizing Mahoney's refusal to debate and his other tactics as "a yellow, skulking, slinky campaign." Mahoney saw Agnew as "the big slob." "Agnew had never done anything in his life. I don't know how he ever got a law degree," he said. In one of his harshest speeches, Agnew, his voice hoarse with emotion, described Mahoney's platform as "a two-pronged devil's pitchfork based on incompetency and bigotry, which he brandishes about while laughing to himself and waiting to pick the bare bones of Maryland." That was the level on which the campaign rushed to its conclusion. The Agnew staff was now genuinely concerned. On the advice of an out-of-state professional campaign consultant, Agnew dropped all pretense of discussing any other issues and focused solely on the Mahoney candidacy and its slogan.

On November 8, 1966, Maryland voters turned out in greater numbers than in any previous gubernatorial election. More than 900,000 people were attracted to the polls, and enough of them were distressed by the racial implications of Mahoney's campaign to give Agnew the office. Agnew's margin of victory was 81,775 votes, just about the size of the Negro vote in Baltimore City, and almost exactly the vote by which the Nixon-Agnew ticket lost the state in 1968, only two years later.

Baltimore County, the area of the state that knew him best, voted against him.

Within hours of the victory, Agnew was being hailed as "one of the Republican party's rising stars." His victory was regarded as a significant setback to the theory of a white backlash. But it had been a near thing. In the eight weeks of the general election campaign George Mahoney had learned how to draw upon that untapped resource Agnew was later to call "the great silent majority." Perhaps if Mahoney had been nimble enough and shrewd enough to make use of this resource while appearing to be above it rather than of it, Agnew's political career might have come to an end. It is, of course, ironic to note that within two short years, Agnew himself would play the role of a George Mahoney on a national level, ferreting out the Wallace votes that the moderates of both major parties disdained.

Mahoney himself was in fact no more of a racist than Agnew was a freethinking liberal. They both took opportunist positions in the 1966 race. Mahoney was stopped not by Agnew but by mobilization of all those who were appalled by the callousness of his campaign and by the kinds of supporters who had rallied around the gimmick of his slogan. Agnew, for his part, had proven little about himself as a politician, campaigner or political personality. Those who were determined to stop Mahoney could not have cared less who Agnew was or what kind of man he was; in their minds only a member of the American Nazi party could have been more of a threat than Mahoney.

The election had not tested Agnew's personal appeal, although the indications were that his margin of victory could have been far greater. He had won no real constituency of his own—liberals did not belong at his side and blacks were soon pushed away. He had not won supporters; he had been used by his supporters to combat George Mahoney. Agnew had merely been available in the right place at the right time. George Mahoney had made Spiro Agnew governor of Maryland.

8 AGNEW HAD WON the full support of the black population in his race for the governorship because of the blatantly racist campaign of his opponent. But in the first few months of his term, black leaders increasingly came to feel that he was not reciprocating for that support. On May 4, 1967, the Reverend Marion C. Bascomb, whose original estimation of Agnew had been formed during the Gwynn Oak affair, publicly expressed the growing black discontent before a meeting of the Interdenominational Ministerial Alliance. Bascomb ticked off a lengthy bill of complaints: (1) Agnew had failed to support a strong open housing bill; (2) Agnew had given an "open-arms welcome" to George Wallace to enter the Maryland presidential primary; (3) Agnew was trying to dictate the direction the civil rights movement should take; (4) Agnew was not available to alliance members who wanted to meet with him.

Bascomb noted that the alliance had worked hard for his election after Agnew had "sought out" black support: ". . . he made numerous promises which would have, if implemented, improved the relationship between the black community and the white power structure." Agnew had promised that his door would always be open to the alliance, yet, Bascomb said, it was becoming increasingly difficult to reach him even by telephone.

Perhaps most significantly, in light of later developments, Bascomb complained about Agnew's meddling concern with the internal policy decisions of the civil rights movement. "We are further disenchanted," Bascomb said, "by the governor's attempt to tell us what we can speak out for or against and how what we say will affect the progress of civil rights. We do not like to keep quiet about Vietnam." Martin Luther King and

Stokely Carmichael, national chairman of the Student Non-violent Coordinating Committee (SNCC), were then stressing the "racist" war in Vietnam and its drain on financial resources that might otherwise have been used to combat domestic problems; this was not a subject that had yet been taken up by the black leaders Agnew professed to admire, men such as Roy Wilkins of the National Association for the Advancement of Colored People (NAACP) or Whitney Young, Jr., of the Urban League.

Six days after the Reverend Mr. Bascomb's speech before the Ministerial Alliance, Agnew, speaking at a testimonial dinner for a state senator, chose to turn from his discussion of state politics to launch an attack on Stokely Carmichael. "He is one of the most irresponsible people to have entered the national political scene," the governor said. "If there are Negroes to admire they are the Roy Wilkinses and the Whitney Youngs. We must draw the line between the responsible leaders and the nuts." He added that he was speaking out, against the advice of "Negro friends who have supported me" because public officials had a duty to confront forces that were confusing people, even at the risk of sacrificing their "political livelihood."

There was at that time considerable disarray in the ranks of black leaders. A year earlier Carmichael's often repeated slogan, "Black Power," had finally come to national attention. The phrase represented neither black racism, black separatism nor a repudiation of nonviolent tactics, but it was taken to mean all of these things. Martin Luther King publicly repudiated the term in itself because he thought it had unfortunate connotations, but he embraced wholeheartedly Carmichael's concepts. In September 1966, Carmichael explained the term at length as a strategy for self-help, a call for black unity in order to facilitate the use of political and economic pressure to achieve an open society. It meant getting forceful representation in the halls of government. And it spoke of the need for a coalition of blacks and poor whites. As for guns, Carmichael asserted the right of blacks as well as whites to own them; maintained the hope that "black power" programs would make them unnecessary, but that the responsibility for violence lay in the white community. The issue of violence revolved around the question of self-defense; Martin Luther King's position, of course, rejected violence even in self-defense.

The civil rights struggle had changed considerably since Agnew's experience in the Gwynn Oak case. In the face of talk that Negroes might retaliate in kind for such acts of previous impunity as the murder of Medgar Evers, the shotgunning of James Meredith, and school and church bombings by the score, the merely disruptive tactics of Martin Luther King began to look positively attractive. But King was the original activist; although nonviolent, he was nonetheless militant. He lined up closer to Carmichael and to CORE's Floyd McKissick than to such moderates as Wilkins and Young, who drew up a moderate position paper on "black power" that King refused to sign. A prudent white public official in a state whose black population was in the hands of moderate leaders would have done well to stay out of this internal debate over tactics and goals. But staying out of controversy was not Agnew's way then any more than it is now.

Carmichael may have seemed to Agnew a rabble-rouser of no substance, but he had demonstrated his courage and abilities before being chosen national chairman of SNCC. He had formed the Black Panther political party in Lowndes County, Mississippi, had headed a registration drive that brought nearly four thousand new black names to the rolls and, although ultimately unsuccessful in electing any candidates, had stuck it out in that toughest of regions despite the shotgun deaths of at least two of his workers. As a result, he had his credentials in the eyes of black America, even though they might not be recognized by white America. Agnew's remarks were therefore a two-edged sword. He forced moderate black Marylanders, who had otherwise been publicly silent, to come to some kind of defense of Carmichael. At the same time, he fed the fears and racist beliefs of a substantial segment of the state at a crucial political time. An open housing bill had been passed by the state legislature, with Agnew's backing, but it was being forced to a public referendum by segregationist elements that hoped to kill it. Negroes needed white support to defeat the referendum. But despite these arguments for silence, Agnew impulsively spoke out.

That speech, on May 10, 1967, set a pattern in regard to

activists that Agnew has maintained for the rest of his political career to date. Regardless of the appropriateness of timing, he will lash out in strong language, reveal that he has been advised against doing so, and offer the opinion that his remarks will be politically costly but that he must rise above politics to express them. It is almost a ritual. After Bascomb's talk on May 4, the Ministerial Alliance continued to press for a meeting with Agnew and finally, on July 12, got to see the governor. The meeting was closed to the press. Afterwards, newsmen were informed that nothing "newsworthy" had occurred other than the governor's promise to maintain better communication with the group. Something far more "newsworthy" had occurred, however. Governor Agnew had been informed about a planned visit of H. Rap Brown to Cambridge, Maryland, and members of the alliance had had some suggestions as to how the governor might handle that visit. Agnew would choose to ignore those suggestions.

Cambridge is a town of about 14,000 people, one-fourth of whom are black. It is on the Eastern Shore of Maryland, that peninsula cut off from the rest of the state by the Chesapeake Bay; it is an area with a physical existence, a provincialism, and a southern orientation of its own. There had been civil rights demonstrations in 1962 in Cambridge. In 1963, further demonstrations had led to real trouble, shootings, and face-to-face confrontations between Negro marchers and National Guardsmen and state troopers. The situation had eventually been brought under control, in part through the efforts of the then U.S. Attorney General Robert Kennedy, but the underlying tensions still existed.

Rap Brown showed up in Cambridge on July 24. His visit had been announced with crudely fashioned posters stuck in store windows and on utility poles. About 350 persons, by newsmen's estimates, ringed Brown as he stood on the hood of a parked car in the Negro Second Ward and began his speech at 9 P.M. It was a speech that was going to have a long life.

The *Sun* quoted Rap Brown as saying, "It's a time for Cambridge to explode, baby. Black folks built America and if America don't come around, we're going to burn America down. I don't know who burned the school down [in a previous fire in a Second Ward school], but you should have burned it down long ago. Then you should have taken over the new elementary school on the other side of town. You better get yourselves some guns. The Man is out to get you. We're not rioting, we're rebelling. That's what's going on."

After the speech the crowd wandered away. About 11 P.M. some gunshots were heard in the Second Ward. Fifteen minutes later, a patrolman answering a call in the ward was struck in the face, arms and hand with shotgun pellets. By 2 A.M. the Pine Street Elementary School was on fire. Cambridge firemen arrived ninety minutes later but refused to fight the blaze. Eventually, ringed by Negroes as a shield against snipers, they attacked the fire, but by that time it was widely out of control. By morning seventeen buildings had been destroyed or damaged, including eleven businesses and the school. The city was occupied by one hundred state troopers, quickly followed by six hundred National Guardsmen. Among the five persons injured was Brown himself who had been treated for shotgun pellet wounds in his face and then, apparently, had left town.

Cambridge police and Dorchester County officials charged Brown with "inciting a riot" and "encouraging to burn" and the FBI, armed with a federal warrant that avoided the necessity of extradition proceedings, began a nationwide hunt to capture him for prosecution in Maryland.

Cambridge cooled down under the patrol of the guardsmen. Agnew, after a tour of the five-block area of devastation, held a news conference and denounced Brown as a "rabble-rouser" responsible for the violence. He called Brown a "professional agitator whose inflammatory statements deliberately provoked this outbreak of violence." He also said, "I have directed the authorities to seek out H. Rap Brown and bring him to justice. Such a person cannot be permitted to enter a state with the intention to destroy and then sneak away leaving these poor people with the results of his evil scheme."

Agnew later was to acknowledge that these remarks were "visceral" rather than "judicious." Brown, at this writing, has not come to trial (and may be dead), so the question still remains as to whether or not he could receive a fair trial in the atmosphere created by Agnew's public finding of his guilt. The remarks were extremely unhelpful, however, in calming a community with a turbulent recent history. The Dorchester County state's attorney would shortly be quoted as saying in an even more injudicious statement that Stuart N. Wechsler, a white member of the Baltimore chapter of CORE, would be shot if he entered Cambridge again. Later, the state's attorney would deny the statement while, in effect, repeating it in his denial: "Anybody who's going to riot and burn and loot in our town is going to be shot if we can shoot him. We cannot condone this lawlessness. They cannot tack the label 'civil rights' on this sort of action."

A few days later, the governor issued a tempered statement acknowledging the just grievances of "our Negro citizens" and setting forth a preventive policy of prior restraints to forestall what he believed was the cause of the Cambridge devastation.

"It shall now be the policy in this state," Agnew said, "to immediately arrest any person inciting to riot and to not allow that person to finish his vicious speech. All lawbreakers will be vigorously and promptly prosecuted." Inciting to riot is a common law crime in Maryland. As later spelled out by the governor, local officials would be advised by the state's attorney general as to when the policy could be used. The *Sun* papers endorsed Agnew's move, but William B. Kunstler, Brown's lawyer, said the next day that such on-the-spot arrests would be a clear violation of the U.S. Constitution. Agnew also announced that he had named a group of eleven whites and ten Negroes to find cures for Cambridge's racial problems—once again the response to a crisis was the formation of a committee.

Agnew's full statement was a clear exposition of his approach to governmental handling of demonstrators. Here are some significant passages:

> In the first place, it is evident that there is ample cause for unrest in our cities. There is still discrimination and, in too many cases, there are deplorable slum conditions. . . . The gains recently made, while good, are not enough. I believe that responsible militants within the Negro leadership should use every means available to place legitimate pressure on those in authority to break the senseless and artificial barriers of racial discrimination. But legitimate pressure—the power of the vote—the power

of organized political, economic and social action—does
not give any person or group a license to commit crimes.

Burning, looting and sniping, even under the banner
of civil rights, are still arson, larceny and murder. There
are established penalties for such felonies, and we cannot
change the punishment simply because the crime occurred
during a riot. The laws must be consistently enforced to
protect all our people. If an angry man burns his neighbor's house, or loots his neighbor's store, or guns his
neighbor down, no reason for his anger will be enough
of an excuse.

. . . the problem-solving conference must be reserved for
those who shun lawlessness, who win their places at the
conference table by leadership that builds rather than
destroys.

The problem-solving must be done by constructive
militants such as the Wilkinses, Kings, Youngs and Ran-
dolphs—not by the Carmichaels, Joneses and Browns. But
it should include the younger responsible leadership as
well as older, more established leaders. Responsibility is
the yardstick.

It shall continue to be my firm policy to do everything
possible to provide jobs, good housing and better educational opportunities for the poor and underprivileged,
both Negro and white, in Maryland. I will meet with any
responsible leaders to discuss the problems that confront
us. I will not meet with those who engage in or urge riots
and other criminal acts as weapons to obtain power.

Following its night of violence, Agnew characterized Cambridge as "a sick city"; when he named the committee to seek
its cure he stated that the city had suffered from "a completely
obvious reluctance to improve some of the most irritating conditions in Negro community." Three aides, including Dr.
Gilbert Ware, the only black on his staff, were assigned the
responsibility of bringing about some semblance of harmony in
the town. After token success in forming a human relations
commission and getting a few local civic and religious leaders
interested in the problem of improving race relations, Agnew's
representatives withdrew and Cambridge was left to solve its

anguishing problems in its own way. To Agnew, the restoration of law and order was a state problem of immediate concern with an obvious means of solution—the exertion of massive police force. The elimination of de facto segregation, even when state laws were involved, did not lend itself to immediate solutions, and did not stir him to imaginative uses of his office. He seemed to believe that segregation would eventually succumb to Time, or Good Will, without the exercise of state or local governmental power.

Two incidents surrounding the events in Cambridge make clear the limits of Agnew's commitment to improving the lives of black citizens. Four days before Cambridge went up in flames, he held a two-hour meeting with Roy E. Wilkins in Annapolis. Wilkins had been contacting the governors of all the states to emphasize a recent federal court decision which made the states fully responsible for ensuring job equality on all public contracts. Wilkins wanted all states to prohibit any official from entering into any publicly financed construction contracts if discrimination existed either in the building trades unions employed by the contracted companies or within the companies themselves. Agnew said he was impressed with Wilkins' "reasonable and unemotional" manner, and the following December he signed an executive order detailing a "code of fair practice" similar to what Wilkins had urged; it depended for its effectiveness, however, on the prestige and influence of the governor's office and carried no penalty, such as the withholding of funds, to force compliance. Six months after the order was signed, Troy Brailey, a Baltimore state delegate and national director of the American Negro Labor Council, objected that nothing had been done in the previous six months to enforce the code of fair practice. It was not lost on Maryland Negroes that while a Rap Brown is deplored, a Roy Wilkins is ignored.

The second incident involved a Baltimore job program. Two days after the Cambridge fires, Agnew journeyed to Baltimore to meet with Mayor McKeldin and then, at a joint news conference, to announce an "immediate crash program" of providing jobs in the city's black ghetto. The two men pledged both state and city funds to the effort. The plan was described amid expressions of great concern that the racial unrest in Detroit (where the large riot of that summer had not yet subsided) and elsewhere in the nation might spread to Maryland. In a separate news conference earlier, and again in the joint conference, Agnew insisted that the job program was possible only because the city Negroes had shown such restraint so far—and warned that it could not continue if violence erupted. This carrot of a program was the extent of his efforts to improve the position of Baltimore blacks in 1967—and even that effort was made at the instigation of Mayor McKeldin and with the torches of Cambridge as a frightening incentive to action.

A final, startling postscript to the Cambridge crisis was offered by Walter Lively, the Baltimore civil rights militant. In deploring the heavy show of force used to put down the Cambridge troubles, Lively claimed that by suppressing the Cambridge blacks Agnew was "seeking a national position in the Republican party and pushing for the vice presidency." If there was anything more to Lively's charge than an eerie kind of prescience, then the subsequent Baltimore city riots of 1968 would provide an even better setting for a thrust into the national limelight.

9 SOME EVENTS in a man's life are important because of their effect upon the course of history or upon the character of the man himself; other events, even unimportant ones, can be of significance for what they reveal to others about a man. The student protest that took place in late March and early April of 1968 at Maryland's Bowie State College, a series of events climaxed by direct confrontation with Governor Agnew, was not in itself of particular importance; but the situation was so clear-cut, so free of extraneous issues, that it can stand as a laboratory test of Agnew's responses when faced with social protest.

Bowie State College was 102 years old in 1968. A four-year, liberal arts college for Negroes, it was part of the state college system and was controlled by the board of trustees of the state colleges. Its sixteen run-down buildings were located on an 187-acre campus just north of Bowie, Maryland, not far from Washington, D.C. At the time of the protests, the student body numbered 595.

The protests began on a low key. Student discontent with bad food, deteriorating dormitories and other substandard conditions had risen to such a degree that afternoon classes were suspended on March 26 while the college president, Dr. Samuel L. Myers, discussed the complaints at a mass meeting. The grievances among the students were not new ones. Two years earlier there had been a one-day boycott at Bowie, the first in its history. The boycott led to a study by the state board of trustees that confirmed the physical deterioration of some of the buildings—faulty heating plants, leaking radiators and showers, exposed pipes, cracked plaster and peeling paint. The student grievances were further backed up by a report concluded one week before the start of the 1968 protests, indicating that 75 per cent of the buildings (including one built as recently as 1966) were seriously enough infested with termites to cause structural damage if, indeed, damage had not already occurred. This report had not yet been released at the time of the protests, but it substantiates the general deterioration of the Bowie physical plant. The 1966 study by the trustees was to have led to remedies for the deterioration—but nothing had happened. In 1967, when Dr. Myers took office as president, the trustees had pledged that Bowie would receive the attention it needed—but nothing had happened.

The day following the mass meeting with Dr. Myers, therefore, the Student Government Association led students in what they called "a passive demonstration" which interrupted normal class routines although the school remained open. A six-page list of grievances was circulated which charged the state with scrimping in its support of the school. The students had the sympathy of Dr. Myers, who told the press the students were "right" in attempting to dramatize the substandard conditions.

Governor Agnew sent an aide, Charles G. Bresler, to Bowie. Bresler told the students to rely on the "orderly processes of government," but since those processes had produced no results in two years' time, the students, who had suspended classroom activity, proceeded with a full boycott.

At this stage, Governor Agnew remained personally aloof from the problem. During his press conference the next day, attention was focused on the coming presidential primaries. (Agnew, who had been embarrassed a few days before by the withdrawal of Rockefeller from the race, was planning to lunch with Richard Nixon on the 30th). But when the matter of Bowie was finally broached, Agnew explained his position. He began by saying that he was "concerned." "But," he went on, "one thing I am completely aware of is this: students always have objections to the way colleges are run. I doubt if we'll ever change that. Our problem is to make certain that we properly assess their objections and make changes where they are indicated, but don't overreact. I don't think we're going to overreact in this case."

On four occasions reporters brought up the matter of Bowie and each time, regardless of the nature of the question, Agnew restated his belief that the situation was not his problem: "it's a college problem . . ."; "it is a college matter that I would expect him [Dr. Myers] and the board of trustees of the state colleges to take immediate steps to clear up and clarify"; "I think you'll remember that we, in our supplemental budget, gave a considerable amount of additional money to the state college system and we left it completely within the prerogative of the trustees as to how that money was to be spent. So again this doesn't involve a judgment of the governor's office . . ."; "I don't consider the Bowie State problem to be in any context a racial problem . . ."; "I don't believe the governor's office should be in each one of these disputes that arises with respect to either colleges or other workers; otherwise, I would have my staff running out to hear grievances aired among thirty thousand-odd state employees and they wouldn't get anything else done. I did it this time because of Dr. Myers' basic newness and unfamiliarity with the situation. . . ."

The inaccuracy of some of these statements was clear even as Agnew spoke; others, he himself would contradict by subsequent action. To begin with, the situation was unquestionably a racial one. Bowie State College had been integrated to some extent, but it remained predominately black. Many of the substandard conditions at the college were the result of neglect during the years when it was entirely black. The kind of subtle discrimination exercised through the withholding of funds from a state institution had been shown to exist at one black state college after another during the 1960s, even though Agnew might choose to ignore it. Furthermore, it would not have been a usurpation of the authority of the board of trustees for Agnew to indicate a personal sympathy for the students, or to promise to do what he could to help them. Clearly, the "orderly processes of government" did not include the participation of Governor Agnew.

That night, having failed to elicit the governor's direct attention, about 150 students, one-fourth of the student population, joined a "sleep-in" in the sixty-year-old, termite-infested administration building. A food collection was begun to support a boycott of the college cafeteria. And Dr. Myers publicly admitted that he "sympathized" with the students.

On Friday at 7 P.M., the students took control of the campus, including its telephone switchboard. They turned on all the lights and all the water faucets in the college buildings, but did not inflict any physical damage to the property. On Saturday, in response to a request for help from Dr. Myers, Governor Agnew ordered a force of 200 state police onto the campus, even though the use of police had already proved to be provocative in other college disturbances. The students at Bowie were not rioters, however; they were demonstrators, trying to make a point that the governor, at least, obviously did not want to grant them. The student leaders, deciding against such alternatives as inviting arrest or barricading themselves in the buildings, which were already tested campus tactics, agreed to cease their demonstration.

The restraint shown by the students in these circumstances was not reciprocated by Governor Agnew, who issued a hardline statement on the situation that evening. The student leaders had pulled back from a tactical position which they, and not the governor, had commanded; apparently taking this as a sign of victory, Agnew indulged in some verbal breastbeating.

> Today's events at Bowie State College should amply demonstrate that this administration has no intention of yielding to the demands and threats of those who would take matters in their own hands and attempt to run the state government.
>
> It is unfortunate that students, who no doubt have legitimate grievances, came under the spell of outside agitators and sought to redress these grievances through occupation of the college administration building and denial of access to the campus, even to the college president. This was an intolerable situation—to the college administration, to the board of trustees and to me. I am glad that it has been relieved without the use of force. But force was present in the state police that I sent to the campus today and force would have been used had the need arisen.

Agnew announced he had prepared a proclamation closing down the college indefinitely and that he was prepared to issue it if further trouble erupted. He said that he would consider discussing the student grievances only after the students had returned to "normal campus life," which included putting an end to the classroom boycott, and he denied reports that he already had made plans to meet them during the coming week. He ended with this peroration:

> It is time that public officials in this country stop yielding to pressures and threats and intimidations by those who would take the law into their own hands. I certainly don't intend to yield to such pressures, and I hope that this is clear from today's events at Bowie.

It was an angry, defiant speech, but the students, fortunately, did not rise to the bait. Instead, they agreed to resume classes on April 2, a Tuesday, and to take no further immediate action. Roland Smith, Jr., the twenty-two-year-old student government president, said, "We are no longer demanding a meeting with the governor or issuing ultimatums." They were "respectfully requesting" the governor and trustees to implement the long-sought reforms.

That same Saturday, Attorney General Francis B. Burch and two state senators had visited the campus while the boycott was still on. The students were undoubtedly calmed by his return with a larger delegation of state senators to show them the conditions about which the students were complaining. In Maryland, the attorney general is elected independently of the governor and Burch was a Democrat. Perhaps for that political reason, but more certainly for the reasons of character that compelled him to be unremittingly stiff-necked, the governor issued on Monday a short statement pulling the rug out from under any ameliorating effect that Burch's visit might have had. Agnew wanted to dispel the "public misunderstanding" that Burch was visiting the campus at the governor's request. Secondly, he wanted to make clear that, although Mr. Burch "is completely well-motivated and sincere," his visit was being "misconstrued" as "an investigation" when the fact was that the board of trustees was "the only proper agency to investigate complaints" at Bowie. Burch and several more state legislative leaders had meanwhile made a two-hour tour of the campus and expressed "deep concern" over the physical conditions they saw; but it was clear from

Agnew's remarks that he wanted the problem to remain the responsibility of the board of trustees.

Agnew had nailed the situation down so firmly that the student leaders had no room to maneuver and the student body had no reason to hope for the achievement of their goals. The students had mobilized themselves in a dramatic protest that had focused public attention on their grievances and then had wisely disengaged in order to give the state an opportunity to respond; now the governor was cutting them dead, even while the campus still seethed with that built-up energy and determination. Spiro Agnew had virtually declared himself their chief enemy. On Thursday, April 4, therefore, more than one-third of the student body journeyed to Annapolis to see their governor.

The students filed into the main corridor of the State House in the early afternoon. They were told that the governor was not in his office and that even if he were there he would not see them. On a voice vote, the students decided to hold a "wait-in" until Agnew would meet with them. The governor, meanwhile, was in Government House, his official residence, just across a narrow street from the State House. Any word of his presence was kept from the students by orders of the state police, and there he lay low, waiting for the students to leave or to agree to see someone else.

Th students remained peaceful, but they were guilty of a technicality, trespassing on public property after closing hours. After a discussion with several of his aides, Agnew ordered their arrest. Three and one-half hours after the sit-in began, the 227 students walked quietly out of the State House to jail. Apparently fearful of the consequences of his precipitate action, Agnew ordered the college closed, sent back a contingency of state police to secure the campus, and alerted the National Guard for possible duty. Forgotten in his insistent retaliation against the students who had dared confront his authority was Agnew's earlier vow not to overreact.

At 7 P.M. that evening, Governor Agnew held a special news conference on the Bowie situation. Read today, the transcript of that news conference is an extraordinary document. The meeting with the press opened with a long statement in which the governor said that "everything possible was done to avoid the need to make these arrests." (Granting a few student representatives a half hour of his time was not apparently in the realm of the possible.) Agnew went on to speak of the general complaints at the college, "which I am the first to admit need great improvement." (It was, however, the first time he had fully admitted it.) "I did not refuse to respond to these complaints," Agnew said, explaining that he had "immediately dispatched" one of his "top staff people" who had spent "a whole day" at the college explaining the aims of the administration. (This top aide was, of course, Charles Bresler, who had informed the students that they should rely on the "orderly processes of government.")

"There are two things that bear emphasizing," the Governor said. "Point Number One: This is not, repeat not, a racial dispute but a dispute between students and college authority. Point Number Two: My refusal to knuckle under to the demands to [sic] students is not a point of personal pride with me, but pride and respect for this democracy and the law and the office of governor of this great state."

Among the distortions and exaggerations of the governor's statement, it was the opening paragraph which the newsmen jumped on most quickly. Agnew said:

> This afternoon I had to make a very hard decision. As hard as the decision was, the need to make it was crystal clear. Very simply the issue was whether or not to excuse and thereby condone a deliberate flouting and defiance of law, and the decision was hard because it involved nearly three hundred young people and their arrest. Young people who confused provocation with principle— who were deliberately inflamed by outside influences, influences which all too often thrive on chaos and disrespect of the law.

The first question from the press corps was directed to this paragraph: "Governor, who are these outside agitators—outside influences—these dangers that you spoke of?"

Agnew answered, "Well, I think you know them as well as I—you've seen them functioning. I'm referring to certain members of the NAACP. . . . I'm referring to the Howard University students, who have no business on the Bowie State campus. . . . Those are outside influences. I don't consider them to be good outside influences. Mrs. Rice from the Prince George's County NAACP. . . ." At a point in the history of the civil rights movement when the nonviolent but militant tactics of Martin Luther King were being challenged by the more militant approach of the Congress of Racial Equality; when the Student Nonviolent Coordinating Committee had devolved, under the increasing militancy of Stokely Carmichael's influence, into the hands of H. Rap Brown, of the revolutionists; and when all of these organizations were finding themselves balked by whites on one side and prodded by the even more extreme Black Panthers on the other, Agnew evoked the specter of the National Association for the Advancement of Colored People, whose firm commitment was to the achievement of progress in the courts rather than in the streets, and whose members were almost alone in holding fast to the ideal of justice through law.

And what of the "deliberate flouting and defiance of law"? Agnew spelled that out in this statement, unasked. "I'm fully aware that these students have been orderly in their disorder," he granted, "but I do not find that an excuse for breaking the law. The law is clear. . . ." And he cited it, Article 27, Section 577A of the Public General Laws of Maryland:

> Any person refusing or failing to leave a public building or grounds, or specific portion thereof, of a public agency or public institution during those hours of the day or night when the building, grounds, or specific portion thereof, is regularly closed to the public . . . shall be guilty of a misdemeanor, and upon conviction thereof shall be fined not more than $1,000, or imprisoned for not more than six months, or both. . . .

"I want to say that I consulted the Attorney General about this law before I took the action I took in making these arrests, and he concurs with me that the arrests are proper," Agnew concluded.

The newsmen left to call in the story. And over the phone most of them learned that the wire services were clogging the teletypes with a bigger story—Martin Luther King had just been assassinated.

The next day, Agnew held a hastily arranged meeting with the college trustees and immediately announced three belated decisions. Bowie would be given $335,000 to be spent immediately in improving the college's buildings and grounds; a search would be made for an additional $500,000 to renovate one of the dormitories; the college's evening program would be expanded and the number of major undergraduate courses would be increased. In the midst of a crisis largely of his own making, after refusing even to speak to students about the issues, Agnew was offering to buy civil peace; once again, as in the Gwynn Oak affair, he was a day late. "We're not making any concessions," he said as he listed the proposals. "The money would have been spent eventually, anyway."

Even as the governor announced his nonconcessions, public support for the students was growing in reaction to the mass arrests. The NAACP announced it had no intention of getting out of the situation, especially since the students needed legal help. The Baltimore *Evening Sun* found Agnew "stiff-necked" and "trying to make problems go away by 'decree' "; in its view the students were asking for nothing except "a fair deal and decent living conditions." At the University of Maryland, it was announced that student leaders from ten state-supported colleges had formed a protest coalition which would point to Bowie as "the epitome of lack of state support." But Agnew only repeated that he would be "increasingly nonresponsive" to student pressure.

College protest demonstrations were hardly a new phenomenon at the time of the Bowie incident. They had been occurring with greater and greater frequency across the country since the Free Speech Movement had erupted in 1964 at the Berkeley campus of the University of California; the most recent demonstration had occurred only days before at nearby Howard University in Washington, D.C. A month earlier, President Johnson's National Advisory Commission on Civil Disorders had issued its massive report (known as the Kerner Report) detailing the frustration of the black community in the face of "pervasive discrimination" and the snail-like pace of what Agnew would have called the orderly processes of government. Widely discussed in the press, the Kerner Report had also noted that in half the disorders it studied, the "final incident" before the outbreak of violence involved police action. Gives the background of experience and analysis provided by other college disturbances and by the findings of the Kerner commission, there was no excuse for the hard line taken by Governor Agnew in the Bowie incident. For even if the experience of the increasingly violent mid-sixties did not provide specific tactics to pursue when dealing with protests, it certainly made clear the kinds of attitudes that inevitably led to trouble. Caution and diplomacy, at the very least, were called for, not the arrogance and belligerence shown by Agnew.

Other public officials had failed as Agnew did in the Bowie incident; many would continue to fail. But most had been and would be faced with far more volatile situations. For if ever, in the violent sixties, a public official was confronted with a "reasonable protest," it was at Bowie College. The issues were simple and specific; the student grievances real and undisputed; the actions of the students deliberate, clearly defined and widely supported; and the prevailing attitude on the campus was shared by students and the administration. The protest was designed to dramatize student grievances. The forms the protest took were legitimate, responsible, firmly controlled and led by officially recognized student leaders, nonviolent at all stages, demonstrably responsive to official overtures, and *legal,* except in two instances when students, at most, were guilty of technically trespassing on public property.

It is possible that even Agnew realized that he had made a mistake, for a month later, in a somewhat similar situation, he reacted very differently. The students at Maryland State College, which, like Bowie, was an almost totally black institution, had become disturbed over the discriminatory practices of local businessmen. When two students were refused service in a local restaurant, the students arranged a meeting with businessmen and local authorities, but it proved to be unsatisfactory. Eventually there were two days of demonstrations, including a downtown march of five hundred students and a mock funeral for the death of "injustice" beneath the town's only traffic light. In the meantime, their unrest stirred other fears and a cross was found burning not far from the campus. At the same time, in Salisbury, about fifteen miles to the north, racial trouble having erupted over the shooting of a Negro deaf-mute, a state of emergency had been called and nine hundred National Guardsmen, reinforcing four hundred state troopers, had just taken over the town.

Perhaps it was the trouble in Salisbury that dictated his actions, or perhaps it was the lesson of Bowie, but Agnew, in a surprise move, called upon Maryland State College student leaders to come to Annapolis to discuss their grievances with him. As fellow students demonstrated in Princess Anne County, sixteen students and some faculty members met with Agnew for ninety minutes. After the meeting, a student spokesman said there would be no more demonstrations. "We have achieved our goals," he said, "and we are very, very pleased with the outcome of the talks." Agnew himself described the meeting as "one of the most productive I've ever been in." He described the students as "reserved, although forceful and dynamic" and said they had made no "unreasonable demands of this administration" but had "responded forthrightly" to his pledges to act. The students had complained of the college's physical condition and curriculum, in addition to discrimination in community housing, employment and public accommodations.

Agnew said he had called the meeting because he had been told that "trouble" could result from the protest. And, in the only acknowledgment of its kind made in the face of repeated racial explosions, he said, "It seemed to me a most unfortunate situation to allow to occur without some affirmative effort to stop it." And so Maryland State, unique in Agnew's administration, demonstrated its grievances without finding itself delivered into the hands of the National Guard.

At a press conference, Agnew was asked bluntly if his approach toward Maryland State was not, in fact, an indication that he had second thoughts about the manner in which Bowie State was handled. "I'd do the same thing over again in the Bowie situation," he said implacably, "and, as a matter of fact, if there are outbreaks of violence followed by demands for meetings in this situation, I will not respond to them at all."

Thus, even if he had indeed learned anything from the Bowie State incident, he was unwilling to admit it. And if a judgment was to be based on the events that had occurred during the month of April, between the Bowie and Maryland College incidents, it would be difficult to believe that he had in fact learned anything at all about conciliation and diplomacy.

10 GOVERNOR AGNEW'S autocratic disdain had closed down Bowie State College and delivered it into the hands of the National Guard. His haughty officialism had herded 227 of the students to jail. And now, two days later, in the wake of Martin Luther King's death, black Baltimoreans, in defiance of white law, white order, white economics and white real property, were about to burn and plunder their city.

Agnew's response to the peaceful petitioning of black students led by their elected leaders was to jail them all. His description of the act of remaining in a public building after business hours was "a deliberate flouting and defiance of law." If such peaceful petitioning (which did not become even technically illegal until after the governor's imperious refusal to meet the students) was an affront to Agnew's concept of "pride and respect for this democracy and the law and the office of this great state," then what words could have been forceful enough, repressive enough, punishing enough and vindictive enough to describe the heedless bands of arsonists, rock throwers and looters who dashed through Baltimore's black neighborhoods night after night?

Fortunately, the question goes unanswered. Baltimore would suffer its share of tragedy in the conflagration that swept the nation, but it would be spared the wrath of Agnew.

By foresighted prearrangement which had nothing to do with the personality of the governor, the job of quenching flaming passions and burning buildings was in hands far cooler than his. If the root causes of the four following days of convulsive self-destruction were the intolerances and cruelties of systematic segregation and official unconcern, then Agnew was among those who supplied the matches. But while the

86

city burned, neither by word nor by action was he allowed to add a stick to those flames.

The urban riots of 1967 which had prompted the Kerner Report had also led to the development of detailed plans for the control of such civil disorders in the future. The plans delineated the roles of local, state and federal authorities and agencies, and were coordinated on the federal level. There was general agreement among those who formulated the plans that large-scale riots in any city could not be controlled or suppressed, but that they could be geographically contained, restricting physical damage to the original areas of riot. Attempts to quell civil disturbances by aggressive actions, physical confrontations and the use of firearms had shown themselves to be ineffective and often counterproductive. In addition, they resulted in loss of lives among civilians, including innocent victims of stray bullets, and increased the likelihood of danger, and even death, to policemen, soldiers and firemen. The strategy for containment called for the quick deployment of law enforcement officials in large numbers and the immediate availability of reinforcements from the National Guard and, if need be, the army. Curfews were to be imposed (riots subside in the daytime, boil again at night) and the sale of firearms, alcoholic beverages and gasoline (used in fire bombs) would be prohibited or restricted. Generally, the plans were based on a principle and a probability. The principle was that lives were more important than property. The probability was that civil disturbances would wear out in about four days—at least they had in the past.

Maryland had such a plan and its key figure was General George M. Gelston. General Gelston had a great deal of experience in dealing with civil disorders, and had proved himself an immensely able leader in such difficult situations. He had first come to public attention in the summer of 1963, when, as assistant state adjutant general and second in command of the National Guard, he had been responsible for containing the violence and for negotiating a truce in the first of Cambridge Maryland's racial uprisings. Although the entry of the guard meant curfews and other restrictions, Gelston was aware of personal rights and group rights to protest and picket. The guard in Cambridge in 1963 was a cooling force that protected the demonstrators from white citizens and also from the impatient local police. Gelston gained the respect of the black population of the state and the grudging respect of white authorities who saw the effectiveness of his approach. His approach was simple: avoid forceful confrontations and prevent the peace-keeping force from becoming an issue in the demonstrations, which meant outmaneuvering both demonstrators and local authorities.

Gelston learned early, for example, that court injunctions against demonstrations only bred trouble. They challenged demonstrators to ignore the injunction and provoked the authorities into demanding mass arrests for those who violated the injunctions. And mass arrests, Gelston knew, simply escalated tensions in a way that played into the hands of the demonstrators, creating more pressures on the community which then demanded more repressive measures. He often looked aside at technical violations of the law, to the annoyance of authorities and to the exasperation of the demonstrators whose tactics at the time often depended upon the hard-headed stance of a Bull Connor to give their demonstrations the dramatic impact they sought. It was a disarming strategy whose effect was to keep both sides fixed on the real issues—the social conditions the protesters wanted changed—and not give the authorities a chance to duck responsibility, or the demonstrators the opportunity to shed their own or his soldiers' blood.

Gelston had also been in command during the 1967 troubles in Cambridge, and, far more than Agnew, was responsible for preventing even greater violence from breaking out. By that time, Gelston had become the adjutant general, been elevated to major general, and was in full command of the state's National Guard forces. Because of his experience and success in handling civil rights demonstrations, he assumed personal command of guard units called out in such circumstances. He also was available as an adviser prior to any move to employ the guard, and may, in this capacity, have saved Agnew from even greater blunders than the governor actually managed to perpetrate.

As a consultant to the Kerner commission, General Gelston was one of three police officers singled out for praise by the commission. Drawing on his National Guard experience and upon a brief stint as police commissioner of Baltimore, Gelston had contributed to the development of the Maryland plan to meet civil disorders, and firmly believed in the efficacy of its basic approach. Thus, when Martin Luther King's death was followed within a few hours by the outbreak of violence in Washington, Gelston was fully prepared for a growing crisis. He had demanded, and received, total authority to handle such disturbances.

After the experiences in Detroit, Newark and other cities in 1967, it did not take a great deal of sophistication to recognize the type of incidents with a potential for exploding out of control. The quick outburst of violence in Washington provided an early warning system for cities all over the country, but particularly for Baltimore, whose plan provided for the possibility of a spillover of disturbances from Washington. As it turned out, Gelston and the city were given nearly twenty hours of lead time.

Officials in Annapolis and in Baltimore were extremely tense as reports came in describing the rapid spread of violence across the country. At noon, Baltimore was still quiet. At 2 P.M., police moved uneasily in the area of a street prayer meeting that attracted three hundred people on Pennsylvania Avenue, the heart of the city's black West Side. There was no trouble; in fact, it was impressively calm.

Earlier in the day, Governor Agnew, mindful of the appalling deterioration of his relationship with the state's Negroes, chose to make a public overture to them. It was an extremely patronizing one, however, in retrospect even insulting. He commended Maryland citizens for "admirable restraint" and attached to his praise an announcement that he would hold a meeting in five days with the mayor of Baltimore and "prominent Negro leaders." The purpose would be "for a frank and far-reaching discussion of the problems that have faced this state and this nation." The press release also contained this sentence: "The governor said he considers it especially important, in view of Maryland's reaction to the current national crisis, to move quickly to consolidate gains that already have been made in the civil rights field and to chart a positive course for the future."

It was another automatic twitch of the nerves by a Maryland politician faced with a crisis—an immediate call (prompt action) for a meeting scheduled just far enough in the future to ensure that no precipitate pressures might force some real action. It was proffered to forestall a riot, as if the mindless tumult that threatened would heed such an intangible opportunity as a "far-reaching discussion." Or did Agnew think that those "prominent Negro leaders" were the ones about to trigger the uprising? One thing was clear, even though at the time it may have been overlooked; Agnew was offering a reward for good behavior. Otherwise, why was it "in view of Maryland's reaction to the current national crisis" that "he considers it especially important" to move quickly, to chart a course, to do something? Why in view of Maryland's reaction? Why not in any case? Why not at Bowie? Why not at any time? Why not before the torch threatened the property and life of the city and the future of the state? Why now when at all earlier times such a "frank" discussion was construed by him to be beneath the dignity of the office he held? Perhaps it was simply the language that was flawed and not the intent. But the proposal was helter-skelter in timing and conception as well as language, for it had not even been determined who was to be invited. It was this scurrying to find victuals to throw to the snapping wolves, whoever they might be, that revealed the statement's meretriciousness even without the proof provided by subsequent events. Nevertheless, the statement was for once absolutely free of invective. It mentioned "racial violence" but it did not refer to looting or arson or characterize those who were committing those acts. For Agnew, this, also, was "admirable restraint." For their part, the "prominent Negro leaders" were glad to receive any gubernatorial attention and anticipated the meeting with good faith.

But it was too late to forestall violence. At about 5 P.M. on Saturday, April 6, store windows in East Baltimore were shattered and bands of black teenagers swarmed through the streets. Helmeted policemen converged on the area. Everything happened very quickly. It had begun.

Governor Agnew, fulfilling the requirements of the law, began issuing the formal proclamations committing the National Guard to the defense of the city on Saturday and calling for federal forces on Sunday; other orders were given, imposing curfews and restrictions.

The riot followed its anticipated course, through four terrible nights. There were more than one thousand fires. The city had called upon the assistance of 10,850 soldiers and guardsmen. Four thousand four hundred and seventy-four arrests were made, mostly for curfew violations. With the advice of Fred Vinson, a deputy United States attorney general representing President Johnson, and under the orders of both General Gelston and Lieutenant General Robert H. York, who assumed command when federal troops arrived, the soldiers and guardsmen were deployed with unloaded rifles and did not fire a single shot. Due in no small measure to this restraint, the riot was responsible for only six deaths. Three persons died in fires, one was killed in an automobile accident, one was killed by an unknown individual in a bar, and a man was shot by a Baltimore city policeman. By Tuesday, April 9, the city had regained control of itself. Gradually, over two more days of careful vigilance, the controlling restrictions were lifted. On Thursday the curfew was finally removed.

Governor Agnew had not come to Baltimore during the disorders. He had kept in touch with events by direct telephone to the 5th Regiment Armory in the city. With calm once more restored, he drove north from Annapolis to view the remains, the gutted rowhouses, the sacked business streets, the broken glass, litter, charred ruins, and the disconsolate people.

"I can't understand it. I can't understand it," he said in puzzlement to an aide. "I never did think that Martin Luther King was a good American, anyhow."

11 O N APRIL 11, a Thursday, the day when the Baltimore city curfew was finally lifted, black state legislators, city councilmen, state and city officeholders, ministers, civil rights leaders and civic organization leaders converged on the State Office Building in Baltimore where, on the top floor, the governor of Maryland maintains a Baltimore office. These were the "prominent leaders of the Negro community" who had been summoned together by the governor in telegrams sent out during the riot.

The past six days had been for them a personal tragedy. To them, it had not been "bands of Negro youths" and "Negro teenagers" anonymously smashing store windows, looting businesses and lighting fires, as the newspapers and television had continually reported. It had been their children. It had been their people inflicting the damage and having damage inflicted upon them. It was their neighborhoods that were burned, their families homeless, destitute or arrested and held in jail under high bonds. The city as a political and social structure had suffered and endured the riot, had met its challenge and prevailed. White Baltimore, with the exception of neighborhood businessmen and some property owners, had been largely untouched by the riot or its aftermath, although it had been inconvenienced by it. White Baltimore saw the destruction on television. And most white Baltimoreans who ventured along Gay Street and Eager and Chase streets to confirm for themselves what had happened could not always tell which buildings had fallen victim to the recent pillage and which had been dilapidated wrecks long before the assassination of Martin Luther King.

On top of all the manifold problems of Baltimore's poor black population there were now the aggravated effects of the past week—the material loss, the disruptions to employment and family life and the rebuilding to be done in an atmosphere in which resentment and hatred and frustration hovered over the city like white and black smoke.

The black leaders responding to Governor Agnew's call were a select group. They were "establishment" leaders— elected officials, appointed "token" officials, clergymen, party politicians and civil rights leaders who had been around so long that even white Baltimore resignedly had come to accept them. But they were no less committed to black causes and civil rights because they worked through the system. And they were no less militant because they worked from within with soft language than were the "cutting edges" whose roles compelled them to use loud language on the streets. Even those "token" Negroes, the solitary blacks in a governmental agency, the black executive director of an ineffectual human relations agency, had hung in, taking their lumps from both sides, persisted, and had gained authority inside the establishment, as well as increased their respectability and their influence and support in the black community outside. These were men such as Parren Mitchell, who had held positions on the state's human relations commission and the community action agency; David Glenn of the city's human relations commission; and Homer Favor of Morgan State College—men who could walk as upright on Pennsylvania Avenue as they could in city hall. There were the clergymen who did what Dr. King had done, marching from the pulpit, praying in the streets, and fusing civil rights and their Christianity into a single commitment. These were men such as the Reverend Marion C. Bascomb, who had been active in the struggle to integrate Gwynn Oak Park. And women such as Mrs. Juanita Jackson Mitchell, who headed the state's NAACP; the wife of Clarence Mitchell, the NAACP's Washington lobbyist, she was a civil rights activist whose credentials had been gained over more than two decades.

Only the changing times had gained these people admission into the governor's meeting. In earlier days most of the clergymen and many of the others had been pariahs to white Baltimore, had been constantly challenged as "unrepresentative" of the Negro community, and publicly or privately labeled as troublemakers. Mrs. Mitchell, a lawyer, is probably the most vilified woman in Baltimore history, with the possible exception of Mrs. Madeline Murray, whose plea to the Supreme Court struck prayers from public school rooms. For years, she had gone into courtrooms, public hearings, police review hearings and before quasi-judicial boards to plead for Negro justice and had suffered personal insults and affronts from judges, lawyers, policemen and city and state officials.

The riot was a frightening challenge to them, as well as a threat to the community that they understood perhaps better than anyone else. Never before, in the face of the most outrageous, inhumane public incidents of official brutality—and there had been many such instances—had Baltimore Negroes allowed their deep-seated frustrations and hidden fury and hatred to boil to the surface in a concerted act of retaliation. If the legal weapons that Mrs. Mitchell had forged and the condescending gains that Parren Mitchell and David Glenn had pried loose from white Baltimore had been limited victories slow in coming, still Baltimore blacks had not in the past chosen to accede to any other course. Clearly, things had now changed. The riot was a watershed and might well be a precedent. These hundred or so black leaders had argued, as had black leaders around the country, that they must be granted their victories, visible evidence of progress or else lose their effectiveness with their communities. And who knew, at that point, the meaning of the riot? And who would have the force to pick up the pieces? Behind all leaders of a cause are lesser leaders impatiently straining. And while these "prominent" one hundred would not deny the younger, impatient, energetic, articulate new breed of activists, they were the city's safety screen and moderator, holding the new breed in check and translating their rallying hyperboles into a form that the white community might find not too unreasonable. Who knew what amputations had been performed in the past week, whether the white man's murder of Dr. King had murdered his influence, too, and severed all such "prominent Negro leaders" from the people they desperately were trying to help. If the murder of Dr. King looked like white America cutting itself off from all blacks whatever their prominence, their following, their Nobel Prize, then perhaps the riots meant that the blacks were cutting themselves away from white America, with hatred on both sides and gasoline bombs to match the guns. If this kind of thinking had been speculative, academic, sociological, even political in the past, it was no longer so. Many of the hundred had spent the past five nights on the ghetto streets, protected by special passes from the police and by their blackness from the neighborhoods. They had seen and heard a lot that had frightened and saddened them. They had, in fact, traveled no man's land under the suspicious surveillance of police who would not distinguish civil rights protests from sudden, violent civil disorder, and confronted by the suspicious questioning of their own people, who could not see the virtue of being able to be near The Man when The Man neither talked nor listened to you.

So now the hundred "prominent leaders" were going to see The Man, even with the federal troops still in the city and the cleanup hardly begun, to restore the white-black roads and bridges and lines of communication. They went to the meeting with more trepidation than hope. "I knew it was a bad meeting . . . I told my folks that I shouldn't even go," said Marshall Jones, a Republican black politician. "I said, 'Ted's going to blow it today.' [But the] guy invited you down there—go ahead down there. I said, 'Okay.' I went in there reluctantly."

There was a gauntlet of state troopers leading the meeting room. This meeting of "prominent Negro leaders" was restricted to those selected as such. Walter Lively had no invitation, but went down to the meeting anyway. Lively was a certified and accredited ghetto street leader. Young, articulate and tireless, he had shunned established activist groups to build his own. At the time of the meeting he was director of the Baltimore Urban Coalition and head of U-JOIN (Union for Jobs or Income Now). He had organized mothers on welfare into an activist group that picketed, paraded and petitioned with unceasing insistency. And he had taken that group to Annapolis when Agnew was inaugurated. They had picketed in a pouring rain while Agnew delivered his State of the State address and had finally gained an audience, the first black group to get to the governor. Agnew had seen them only reluctantly, had listened to them impatiently, and nothing had come of the meeting.

Lively was on the streets constantly during the riots, helping in the organization of emergency aid stations and advising and consoling people in the neighborhoods. He had also been arrested when police noticed him at the sites of several fires. But no charges were placed against him and he had been released quickly. It was not the first time police had picked him up. In fact, for a time, police obtained a warrant for him for failing to pay some parking tickets, and held the warrant so they would have a legal justification for arresting him anytime in the future when they wanted to get him out of circulation. Lively did not get into Governor Agnew's meeting, but, as it turned out, he figured in it. In his speech, Agnew would accuse him of having something to do with the setting of eight fires.

Two of those who were invited arrived to tell the governor that they preferred not to attend his meeting. The governor met with them privately. They were not exactly "leaders" of the black community, but they were prominent and they had personal influence. They were John Mackey, a star, and Lenny Moore, a former star, of the Baltimore Colts, two of the best-known black athletes in Baltimore. They told the governor they could be more effective on the streets talking to youngsters and adults if they were not seen consulting with the power structure. Agnew, a fan of the Colts and usually among the crowd at their games, was chatting with the two athletes in another room as the other prominent leaders arrived. The force of state troopers and the screening of the guests was unsettling, an unpleasant reminder of the armed camp that Baltimore had become in the past week. And as they entered the meeting room, the atmosphere thickened. There was the press—reporters from several papers, radio men and television crews with their cameras and lights. It was not to be what they had expected, a private, serious, "frank and far-reaching" discussion, for how could that take place in front of television cameras for immediate telecast that evening, even as federal soldiers still patrolled the city?

The governor had not yet appeared. He was still talking to the two football players. The large audience of prominent leaders of the black community were looking about the room, each one knowing from his own invitation certain others who mi̤ght also be invited, but not sure which other categories of "prominent leaders" the meeting would include. It was not hard to locate the omissions. There were no representatives of CORE or SNCC or local groups such as U-JOIN (Walter Lively's organization) or the Civic Interest Group. The invitations had not only been select, but discriminating, and in a way that would make no sense in the black community, regardless of the governor's rationale. To some in that audience there came a realization like a trap being sprung. Out of that meeting The Man hoped to drive a wedge in the crack between those he considered moderates and those he considered militants. The troopers at the door were guarding the line of demarcation.

Earlier in the year, Robert B. Moore, head of the Baltimore chapter of CORE, had accused President Johnson and Baltimore Mayor Thomas D'Alesandro of planning a "war on the black community" through the campaign against crime in the streets. The police, said Moore, were "the enemy of the black community." The remarks were too intemperate and impolitic for State Senator Clarence M. Mitchell III. Mayor D'Alesandro ranked rather high with the Negro community and with all those black leaders who counted on city hall support for improvements for blacks. President Johnson was the personal source of several much-needed pieces of national legislation. (The senator, who attended Agnew's meeting, would go from there directly to Washington to witness the President's signing of the 1968 civil rights bill.) Senator Mitchell, one of two blacks in the state senate, countered Moore's remarks in a strong statement delivered on the senate floor. Moore, he said, was guilty of "bigotry." In the area in which he operated it was as necessary for Mitchell to make his defense as it was necessary for Moore, in his area of operation, to make the attack. Nevertheless, the exchange attracted black support in both directions and a "black unity" meeting had been held to kill the dispute. The gamut of the civil rights movement had been represented at that meeting, including Black Power leaders, anti-poverty officials and politicians.

The civil rights movement has lived with two white myths since its inception. The first is that, no matter what the issue or where the confrontation with the establishment, "a few ouside agitators" provoke a problem where none existed. The second is that the movement is "split" by a "feud." Both myths stem from the same white hope and belief that there are good Negroes and bad Negroes in the movement, the bad ones being the pushers of unreasonable demands leading to the demonstrations that agitate society. Since every difference in approach is misconstrued by the press and the power structure as a difference in goals, a "split," the movement has always had to defend itself, in fact guard itself, from even minor differences. And so there was no "split" in Baltimore, no crack in which to drive a wedge. But there was, to many of those enchambered in the State Office Building, that cordon of state troopers making the myth of the split a physical reality—and one that would pop into view on the screens of every television set turned to the six o'clock news.

Still the governor did not appear; and now he was late. This had not been deliberate, some vain late entrance to make certain from the start that one hundred prominent black leaders understood who was governor and who were the governed. There was no rudeness intended, not in that lateness nor in any small detail of that meeting. But the black leaders might have felt as they did in fine restaurants when, after a time, it became clear that no one was coming to serve them. They were not aware that Governor Agnew was in conference with two Baltimore Colts. Charles Bresler, the governor's aide in charge of state relations with the federal government and its agencies supplying money for state programs, attempted to fill the delay. Bresler was the aide sent as surrogate by Agnew who had failed to convince the Bowie students to abandon their protest. Now he appeared like a messenger in a Greek play. Marshall Jones, the politician who had not wanted to go to the meeting but decided to, remembers vividly how it went:

> Bresler started the meeting. And this was never recorded. Bresler was starting the meeting talking about how his parents had come to this country for religious reasons; Agnew, Ted's family, [was] second generation Greek, and he had pulled himself up by his boot straps; blacks had come over as slaves; and—you don't hear that

kind of stuff. Hell! Everybody knows what America is. You know? So this was a prelude to what was to come. I knew it was a bad meeting. . . .

And so that was the setting for Governor Agnew's confrontation (the idea of a meeting had died long before) — except for one addition. The governor had been conferring with the heads of all the law enforcement elements just before the meeting (in addition to the conference with the Baltimore Colts) and had decided to bring them along. And so Bresler stopped talking as the governor walked into the room and moved to the front, flanked by Major General George M. Gelston, Colonel Robert J. Lally, head of the state police, and Donald Pomerleau, city police commissioner. Bresler joined the group and Dr. Gilbert Ware, Agnew's black aide and the first black on a governor's staff in Maryland history, moved discreetly or self-consciously, or protectively, to the side of the room, making the black-white arrangement as neat for the television cameras as could be desired by anyone with an eye for showdown. The last fillip was provided by General Gelston, the only man in that row of white power and force with credentials in the black community, a man extremely sensitive to the appearances as well as the substance of civil rights negotiations and confrontations, always cool in temper, warm in personal contact, with no vanity or false pride to stumble over, and a sense of humor that enabled him to ride calmly when his adversaries deliberately intended to provoke him. Gelston, who has since died, was a compulsive storyteller, and would have enjoyed the irony of his cameo role. Standing in front of the room, in view of many who knew and respected him, he found himself with his swagger stick in his hand. With a lapse of regard for the subtleties he habitually attended to, the general placed his stick on the table in front of him.

As General Gelston's swagger stick was placed in view on the table like a gauntlet thrown to the ground, Governor Agnew began his speech. "Hard on the heels of tragedy come the assignment of blame and the excuses. I did not invite you here for either purpose," the governor began, and later it could be wondered if he had paid attention to his own words. His typewritten speech was four pages long when it was handed to the press at the meeting, and three of those pages assigned blame, on outside agitators, on civil rights militants who supported and encouraged the views of the outside agitators, and on the persons before him who refused to repudiate the people he was identifying by name, or inference, or category.

The governor could have said, truthfully, that he had not extended the invitations in order to place blame (since the idea of the meeting preceded the riot) but that he had decided later that the meeting could serve that purpose usefully. The speech was both general and specific in its criticisms and characterizations, slapping on invective with a heavy brush that touched everyone in the black community. He spoke of the public exchange between Senator Mitchell and Moore, the CORE leader, whom he called "a reckless stranger." And he condemned the "black unity" meeting, chastising those who attended it for "breaking and running" to accommodate themselves to "those who depend upon chaos and turmoil . . . those who were not invited here today." Those he had not invited he called "the caterwauling, riot-inciting, burn-America-down type of leader." And he accused those he had invited of meeting in secret and entering into an agreement with "that demagogue" Moore and "others like him." One idea directly following another, Agnew said, "Now, parts of many of our cities lie in ruin," clearly linking the "black unity" meeting with the riot. He referred to Walter Lively as one of the "advocates of violence" at whose "suggestion" and "instruction" fires were lit in the city.

He blamed Stokely Carmichael directly for the outbreak of violence, mentioning that he had been in the city on April 3. On the surface this accusation seems absurdly implausible unless Carmichael was clairvoyant or had foreknowledge of the death of Dr. King on April 4. Actually, Agnew had a more logical theory, one he did not spell out in the speech. Information he had received from the FBI on Carmichael's visit and the presence of Howard University students on the Bowie campus led him to confide to Mayor D'Alesandro that the assassination of Dr. King had prematurely set off the riots, which interfered with the actual plans of a conspiracy that would have been even more devastating.

In the speech, Agnew claimed that Carmichael met with black power leaders and known criminals (this being part of the conspiratorial planning he spoke of to Mayor D'Alesandro), and that these black power leaders had already obtained from Agnew's guests at this meeting the promise that they would not publicly criticize them. Agnew's argument was, in effect, that these people before him had helped cause the riot, and had aided a conspiracy that was responsible for the form of the riot. It is significant, however, that no one was ever arrested or indicted on any charge of inciting to riot or conspiracy even though the state had had a recent case of just this nature and had won it. The state had tried and convicted two white men, Joseph Carroll and Connie Lynch, who had held a rally urging on a white crowd, over loudspeakers, with repetitive chants of "Kill the Niggers; Kill the Niggers," "I hate Niggers" and similar cries.

The prominent Negro leaders did not follow the chain of reasoning in the governor's speech. They simply heard Agnew's characterization of other Negro leaders not present and knew that the trap had indeed snapped shut, and that they had not been invited in so much as divided in. It was as if they had been culled as good specimens for local use while their brothers were to be sold down the river where the work was harder and where there was less concern about how long a darky lived. That very image of slave days did in fact come into some of their minds. Senator Mitchell said, "The comment throughout the community after that confrontation, and it was exposed on TV, was that this was an attempt on the part of the slave master to call in the house slaves and whip them for not being able to make the rest of the slaves stay in line. And this was the comment of the average man on the street. The reaction in the poor white community and the blue collar white community was, 'That Agnew sure is giving them hell, and we sure are glad to see him giving those leaders hell.' "

As Agnew read through his speech, the prominent black leaders listened intently. "I did not invite you here for either purpose [blame or excuses]," he had begun misleadingly. He read four long paragraphs before his intent became clear. "And you ran," the governor said, and the offense became visible on the faces of his audience. They were stunned, and perhaps

mistrusted their own comprehension of what was being said.
But as the words rolled on ("intimidated by veiled threats,"
"stung by insinuations," "Mr. Charlie's boy," "breaking and
running"), the audience began to react. A few at a time and
then many at a time, the prominent black leaders rose to their
feet and walked out. "If you want to talk to us like ladies and
gentlemen, Mr. Governor, we'll stay and listen," said one man,
But the governor, his eyes fixed to his page, read on. Several
people shouted for a "black caucus" outside and more people
left the room. Gene Oishi, reporting the meeting for the *Sun*,
wrote, "A startling aspect of the walkout was that it was staged
by persons generally recognized as forming the moderate segment of the Negro leadership, in fact, hand-picked by the
governor's staff to attend."

The protest was unanimous. But the black leaders each
responded in his own way, according to his own inclination
and personality. About seventy people walked out, their anger
and hurt impelling them to get away from the source of the
insults. But about thirty people stayed. It was as if the group
brought together by the governor, then insulted by him, had
found community and assumed their own responsibilities for
the common good. The Reverend Mr. Bascomb left storming,
then joined with other ministers to march to a nearby church
and confer and respond, just as they had done in crisis after
crisis. Some politicians remained. After all, the seventy who
walked out had made an effective gesture. Perhaps something
could be gained by remaining to placate and negotiate. Mrs.
Juanita Jackson Mitchell, the chief NAACP lawyer in the state,
stayed to plead a case for the defense, her old role once more
in an accusatory white society. She was among the first to reply
to the governor when he had ended his statement.

She, too, deplored violence and racism, as the governor did,
but there was the historical lesson that in the United States
"it is only when there is violence or the threat of violence that
the body politic moves."

Agnew, seated, the judge to her role as lawyer, overruled
her, saying that violence had to stop being the historic course
of the country, "or we're all going to be dead, everyone of us."
And then, suddenly turning accusatory, he changed Mrs. Mitchell from defense counsel to accused, and the scene from trial

to inquisition. "Do you repudiate Rap Brown and Stokely Carmichael?" the governor demanded, "Do you? Do you?" reducing her from a prominent Negro leader to her proper role and place, patiently pleading for justice as white judges joined in sadistic courtroom baiting.

"I don't repudiate any human being," Mrs. Mitchell said. Then, her voice choking with tears, she said, "This city, this government, have made them what they are . . . have made our children burners and looters." But her point was probably lost. Agnew had not been talking about anybody's children. He had been talking about Rap Brown.

There were a few white people in the audience, including Mrs. Mae Gintling, director of a community center in West Baltimore. "You're listening, but you're not hearing," she told the governor. "This is not the time to repudiate people, but causes." Black militants were speaking the mind of the common people, she said, "And you'd better hear it."

"We love you, Governor, we love you," implored State Senator Verda F. Welcome, as if she could change his mind, recall the speech, despite the television cameras that had stored it away for 6 P.M., just as they were at that moment storing away her pleas not to be sold down the river. The meeting continued for two futile hours after the speech, but there was no reconciliation. The governor listened to the arguments and the retaliations and the excuses he said he had not come to hear. Through it all he drew on the personal conviction that he was absolutely right in what he had just done, and right about what he had said. He was as certain about his rightness as he had been when he encouraged primary opposition to Fife Symington in 1962. No arguments were able to persuade him otherwise. He had shown the speech to Dr. Ware, his black staff member, and had been advised not to deliver it. He also had shown a copy of a Rap Brown speech to Senator Welcome and she had refused to repudiate it, so he felt he knew what the reaction to that proposal would be. He had also talked with Mayor D'Alesandro about his speech. D'Alesandro had advised him not to carry out his plan, and when Agnew decided to go ahead anyway, the mayor found an excuse to be somewhere other than at the meeting.

And so, Agnew had heard all the arguments against saying what he did, and he had gone ahead and done it anyway; there was little chance he would back down now. There were to be "no apologies or regrets," he told reporters. "If they had all walked out I would simply be faced with a situation where I would have to find other Negro leaders," he said.

12

Agnew's HARD-NOSED lecture to the prominent Negro leaders he had called together was not merely ill-advised or intemperate, it clearly was dangerous. The city had exhausted itself in the four days of fires, looting and arrests. But tensions were still high, and if the patterns of riots are apparent to some experts, their root nature remains elusive. Until the death of Martin Luther King, the only thing close to a riot in recent years had occurred when the white racists Carroll and Lynch had provoked white youths to range through the streets of East Baltimore beating any Negroes they came upon. Certainly, there was a strong, suppressed streak of violence lurking in the white community. In fact, as the disorders following Dr. King's death developed, white businessmen and city and state politicians angrily began calling upon city hall and upon the governor to get down to business, to stop the lawlessness in the streets, to have the police do to looters what they had always done to burglars or escaping suspects—shoot them on sight. Might not the governor's public rebuke of black respectability give license to angered and vengeful whites who felt a need to retaliate against the black rabble that had thrown their city into disorder? On the other side of the question, Agnew's harsh, recriminatory words might easily have fanned back to life the smoldering embers of riot in the black community.

During the Cambridge disturbances, Governor Agnew had publicly accused Rap Brown of inciting to riot, and he ordered his arrest on those charges; subsequently he had announced a state policy of prohibiting such speeches on pain of immediate arrest. Although it was not a direct incitement to riot, the possibility of a riotous response to Agnew's speech to the black leaders was strongly evident. At the very least, it was an inflammatory speech, and was quickly labeled so by the mayor of Baltimore.

Recognizing the dangers in Agnew's speech, Mayor D'Alesandro had urged the governor not to make it; when his advice was ignored, he immediately moved to mitigate its possible effects by calling a hasty press conference of his own. So that the press and television cameras could reach him without undue waste of time, he held the conference at the 5th Regiment Armory, headquarters of the riot control forces, which were only a half block away from the site of Agnew's meeting.

The mayor is given to unusual candor with the press, especially on issues difficult to resolve. At these times, he reveals, much as Robert F. Kennedy did, his own self-doubts, misgivings and frustrations. The mayor did so now as he explained to the press his reason for calling the news conference.

He had learned, he said, that the governor had planned a "tough statement," a "somewhat inflammatory" statement and that he had called the governor in an unsuccessful attempt to get him to modify the speech. Confronted with that failure, he wanted to make his own position clear. A reporter directed Mayor D'Alesandro's attention to his use of the word "inflammatory." Did he really mean "inflammatory?" The mayor paused to reconsider what he had said. Then he replied, "On second thought, yes. It was inflammatory."

"We should be emphasizing reconciliation and harmony, not divisiveness," he continued. "This is a bad time to say what he said. Most of the people reject the extreme aspects of both sides. I would rather stress the positive approach, not fight among ourselves. Let's get down to the people's problems."

As the mayor made his statement he, too, was flanked with prominent Baltimoreans, each of them white and, if not necessarily known to the man in the street, nevertheless constituting a forceful show that the mayor was not a lonely voice in calling for restraint and conciliation. There was William Boucher III, director of the Greater Baltimore Committee; Francis D. Murnaghan, president of the city school board; Francis X. Gallagher, attorney for the Baltimore archdiocese; Robert Levy, chairman of the board of the Hecht Company department

store chain; James W. Rouse, the land developer who put together the planned city of Columbia, Maryland; and E. Clin-
ton Bamberger, a prominent local lawyer. It was a hastily as-
sembled group, but there were Catholics, Protestants and Jews,
representatives of big business, commerce, the school system
and the legal profession. It was a sufficient contrast to the
soldiers and cops that had surrounded the governor's appearance.

The mayor's speech offered friendship, trust and hope. It
was part plea, part promise and absolutely free of rancor and
recrimination:

> The city and the whole community was hard hit by the
> force of the disturbances, but I believe that it absorbed
> the punch with remarkable resiliency. The vast majority
> of the people, black and white alike, did not participate
> in the disturbances and do not approve of them. We can-
> not permit the disturbances to divide the community into
> two separate camps. I shall not permit the disturbances
> to deter my administration from continuing on the course
> we set approximately four months ago when I took office.
> I said then and I say today that the city of Baltimore is
> confronted by grave economic and social problems. We
> must provide more jobs, better housing, cleaner neigh-
> borhoods, quality education, broader health programs and
> more recreation facilities to all of our citizens, both black
> and white. We must make these programs more accessible
> to the people down in the neighborhoods. And we must
> give the man in the street a greater participation in these
> programs.

Mayor D'Alesandro's statement provides an interesting contrast to Governor Agnew's. D'Alesandro, who was in his late
thirties at the time, had been in office for only four months.
But he had been president of the city council before he became mayor. His father, too, had been mayor of Baltimore,
as well as a U.S. congressman, and young Tommy had been
active in politics and had the opportunity to learn about the
problems of government when he was still a teenager. He had
become mayor with a coalition of white and Negro votes, just

as Agnew had become governor. As a politician and as a government official he found it not only possible, but necessary, to speak of rebuilding without issuing recriminations.

For all of his deep background in machine politics, D'Alesandro has demonstrated over the years a concern with government far deeper than Agnew's. He has, on many occasions, thrown himself into tough battles with the city council in support of something he believed in, even though he faced inevitable defeat. Agnew often has claimed he was putting his political future on the line, but such claims have usually seemed only a rhetorical device. In his farewell address to the Maryland General Assembly after being elected Vice President, Agnew said, "If we were not at all times wise, who can say we were at any time timid." His boldness, however, came in the force of his words, not in programs, nor in terms of the leadership of his tenure as governor.

There is a misconception that Agnew had a good record with blacks and good relations with them until his public chastisement of their moderate leaders following the Baltimore riot. But this was not the case. Nor was Agnew "telling it like it is" as he is fond of saying, for the first time in that 1968 confrontation. It was simply the first time he would do it so spectacularly and with such devastating effect.

As county executive, Agnew was faced with one active disturbance, the demonstrations to integrate Gwynn Oak Park. As governor, he was confronted with a near-riot in the city of Cambridge; demonstrations leading to mass arrests at Bowie State College; demonstrations at Maryland State College; and the full-scale riots in Baltimore. Taken together, they form a substantial record of the man in the face of such crises. What emerges from that record is his rigid abhorrence of direct action tactics, his contempt for demonstrators, his propensity to remain aloof from threatening situations until they have reached the point of explosion, his use of the punitive force rather than the constructive possibilities of his elective offices, and his predictable announcement of some token concession as a last resort and after it is too late. Repeatedly, his public expressions during these crises were provocative rather than conciliatory, personal rather than diplomatic, and, invariably, against the best advice of his friends. The result of this was to make him a party to a dispute that initially did not directly involve him, often making *him* the target of animosity that had originally been directed elsewhere. Neither Agnew nor his policies were at the core of the Gwynn Oak, Cambridge, Bowie or Baltimore city disturbances, but after his intercessions public attention was diverted from the issues to him.

Agnew did not come into office facing a tough racial situation in the state. The state did have serious social and economic problems; segregation was not dying of its own accord, but it was weak enough so that it could have been killed. The state administration could count on strong, influential, white liberal support in Baltimore and in Montgomery County, near Washington, D.C., for every civil rights stand that was taken. The trouble spots on the Eastern Shore had been marked by violent flare-ups in the past and the issues were defined; there would be no surprises of this sort. The city of Baltimore had never had a race riot; during Agnew's term it would be governed by two administrations, both of which maintained extremely cordial relations with the black populace. The most militant civil rights groups were mainly concerned with jobs and public accommodations. The legal weapons needed to win these fights were already at hand, and were being strengthened by both Congress and the courts by an almost unending flow of legislation and judicial decisions.

It was a good and right time for a governor to build a substantial civil rights record without jeopardizing his career. There were already many areas of improvement which were legally mandated; it would not be necessary to lead, only to follow through. Yet the implementation of such mandated changes would accrue to the credit of the governor whose administration coincided with the improvements.

Agnew not only failed to take advantage of this situation; by exacerbating, with his divisive rhetoric, the fears and anger of the white segregationists who already were disturbed by the gains made by the blacks, he actively endangered the forward movement that had been attained. What then was it about this man, who so often restated his moral belief in an integrated society, that prevented him from acting upon the possibilities inherent in the social situation at the time he became governor? What was it that deterred him from helping the black man move toward the integration that Agnew himself insisted was his right? Is Spiro Agnew merely a hypocrite, and a segregationist at heart? If that is the case, he does not appear to be consciously aware of his hypocrisy, or of his segregationist instincts. But there is another possible explanation for his behavior, one that does operate at an entirely conscious level of his mind.

Spiro T. Agnew believes in the Law. Obedience to Law brings Order. Law and Order rule supreme in Agnew's view, and are the undeviating standards by which to judge men's actions both singly and in the mass. The rigidity of his belief in Law and in Order puts him on the side of Law over Justice, for he can no more condone breaking an unjust law than breaking a just law; in fact, such a distinction finds no place in his system of ethics. If the distasteful matter of unjust laws cannot be avoided, he falls back on that other supremacy, Order. Order dictates that the changing of undesirable statutes must wait upon the deliberations of legislative bodies, however long they may take.

This is his code. Yet, when unjust laws are changed, he does not find it easy to adapt to the new laws. They do not quickly become for him Law with a capital letter.

When a state law banning segregation in public accommodations was about to take effect in 1963, Agnew made an appeal to civil rights leaders to "exercise statesmanship and strength," saying, "It is my earnest hope that there will be no outburst of demonstrations, no intemperate haste to test the law and the Supreme Court ruling, no rash actions to jeopardize the advances that are possible." In other words, no concern that restaurant, motel, bar and theater owners obeyed the law.

Similarly, in October 1963, when the head of the Baltimore County Human Relations Commission said of the problems of segregated housing, "There are certain injustices which can only be corrected with legislation now," Agnew abandoned his usual confidence in the efficacy of democratic processes and said, "I don't think this is an area for governmental action at this point. . . . We face a long and difficult problem in educating the general public so that changes from a segregated to an integrated neighborhood will not affect property values. These changes can best be achieved by understanding between the races. . . ." In May 1964, he even rejected a request for a joint study of open occupancy conditions in Baltimore County and the city. Later in the year, as court decisions followed one upon the other in many states upholding new laws banning racial discrimination in home sales and rentals, Agnew continued to insist that open occupancy legislation would invade rights of privacy guaranteed by the federal Constitution. In October 1965, he was still adhering to his opposition to open occupancy legislation, toying with the idea of laws that would ban discrimination in future housing, but not in existing housing, and calling for voluntary efforts to achieve integration.

In the face of this inconsistency toward the supremacy of Law, a civil rights advocate could, however, distinguish a more prevailing consistency, an ultimate belief in the Status Quo as being supra-supreme, above even Law and Order. But we have come full circle, and again the questions must be asked: "Is Agnew a racist?" "What's a racist?" Marshall Jones, the black politician, shot back in response to a question from the author. "I don't know. It means he dislikes black people? . . . Does Ted dislike me? Hell, I don't know. I don't even know how far I want to get into it. The image of the [Nixon] administration is that of being not sensitive to the needs of the poor—black—you know. This is the image. . . . The image is that they're anti-black."

There is another way of looking at the question. It is not necessary to accuse Agnew of being a racist, of being biased against the Negro, to demonstrate that he is biased in favor of the white middle class. Agnew will not accept the black argument that discrimination and its effects led inevitably to disrespect for the law and that riots are not an effort to change the system but rather a symptom of the system's sickness, its chronic injustice. A month after the Baltimore riots, he spoke as follows:

> Intellectual and spiritual leaders hailed the cause of civil rights and gave little thought to where the civil disobedience road might end. But defiance of the law, even for the best reasons, opens a tiny hole in the dike and soon a trickle becomes a flood. . . . And while no thinking

person denies that social injustice exists; no thinking person can condone any group's, for any reason, taking justice into its own hands. Once this is permitted, democracy dies; for democracy is sustained through one great premise: the premise that civil rights are balanced by civil responsibilities.

The problem with the black point of view, so far as Agnew is concerned, is that the blame falls on white America instead of upon the rioters. Governor Agnew made this very point on July 23, 1968, in a speech to a closed session of the National Governors' Conference. The speech was entitled "A Critique of the Kerner Commission Report." Here are some random quotes:

> From the introduction it became clear that the Kerner commission was prepared to indict the American mainstream—black and white—for the riots in our cities.
> These conclusions [of the Kerner Report] put the cause of violence in a socio-economic context rather than a racial one. Yet we know, two out of three Americans below the poverty level are white. This opens the way to new and disturbing questions. Why don't impoverished white Americans riot? Could it be that they know they will not meet with sympathy, that collective white lawlessness will not be tolerated?
> It is not the centuries of racism and deprivation that have built to an explosive crescendo but the fact that lawbreaking has become a socially acceptable and occasionally stylish form of dissent. . . . It was the orderly demonstration of civil disobedience praised and participated in by our nation's civic, spiritual and intellectual leaders that gave impetus to civil disorder.

Governor Agnew repeated most of this speech, with some omissions and some additions, a week later in New York City, where he addressed a conference of the Greek Orthodox Youth of America. There, his language became even harder:

> Civil disobedience, at best, is a dangerous policy, since it opens the path for each man to be judge and jury of

which laws are unjust and may be broken. Moreover, civil disobedience leads inevitably to riots, and riots condoned lead inevitably to revolution . . . [sic] which, incidentally, is a word we are hearing more and more frequently from advocates of black power.

It would occur to a black that there have been, in fact, many instances of "collective white lawlessness" that have gone unpunished, not just scores of lynchings on which local societies turned their backs, but the widely ignored Supreme Court order to integrate schools. What's more, a black would point out, this kind of widespread, officially condoned, national disobedience preceded the use of civil disobedience as a tactic in the black struggle against segregation.

What makes suspect Agnew's voiced adherence to equality before the law is this rejection of civil disobedience, the most effective weapon in the civil rights arsenal, coupled with his own refusal or inability to suggest or support alternatives. In the speech at the National Governors' Conference, he called the Kerner Report's recommendations "surprisingly unoriginal and undramatic," adding, "I for one cannot believe infusing more money into the so-called ghetto is the answer. Our goal should be to eliminate ghettoes altogether, not to build better ones. . . . The term ghetto is a misnomer since it implies forced housing on the basis of race. The common bond of the slum neighborhood results from social and economic far more than physical conditions." The suburban exodus, he said, was not so much a "white phenomenon" as "the route of the educated, the employed and the economically well-off." This is an amazing statement in view of the strict racial covenants that maintain Baltimore County as a white noose around the central city, covenants that were the source of problems for him throughout his terms as county executive and governor.

Agnew, who had opposed open occupancy laws for several years and later reluctantly approved a modified measure, opposes, in this speech, outlays of money for housing and jobs as "short-term and costly." As an alternative, he put forth his plan for "satellite cities," planned communities, racially integrated, with a balance of housing and industry to relieve the urban impaction. Whatever other merits that idea may have, it certainly is not a feasible approach to providing the immediate help the cities now need.

The black leaders of Maryland had been instrumental in Agnew's election to the governorship, although it is true that they had no choice, given the racist nature of George Mahoney's campaign, other than to support Agnew. But many of them had done so with hope. Whatever residue of that hope remained after the Baltimore riots was thoroughly eradicated by Agnew's speech before the meeting of Negro leaders. Those who walked out of that meeting gathered immediately at a local church, and a rebuttal was drafted that would speak for all. It said in part:

> Shocked at the tone and fervor of the governor's remarks, a number of us decided that the meeting had no possibility for constructive action.
>
> Agnew must be made to know that he cannot treat black men and women like children. Agnew must be made to know that all Americans are going to share fully in the fruits of this country. Agnew must be made to know that the old techniques for dividing and conquering will not work. . . . We are shocked at the gall of the governor, suggesting that only he can define the nature of the leadership of the black community.

The following day, others joined Mayor D'Alesandro, the black leaders themselves, and the *Sun* papers, in condemning the speech. Baltimore clergymen led a procession of about eight hundred persons in a "procession of penance" for the shame of racism. Nearly four hundred of that group signed a petition to Agnew saying they deplored his "obvious lack of understanding of the urban crisis." A group of thirty Catholic priests from inner city parishes said the governor's "intemperate lecturing" was "an affront to men and women who have labored for many, many years to rid Baltimore of the evil effects of racism. . . ."

Thirteen days after the meeting, the governor sent a letter to each person invited to the meeting. It asked for their advice, in the form of return letters, on the underlying causes of "the recent disturbances," possible actions that could be undertaken to prevent their recurrence, immediate steps to aid the city's prompt recovery, and suggestions for a future meeting of the black leaders and himself. The letter was so hopelessly out of line with the feeling about Agnew that now existed in the black community that it was largely ignored. It seemed to pretend that no walkout had ever occurred. An aide to the governor said that the letter was not, in fact, an attempt to re-establish contact with the blacks: "Nothing had been, what you would call, broken," he said. For the governor himself did not think of his speech as divisive, but rather as a part of his continuing communication with the black community.

13 BALTIMORE COUNTY IS not a political kindergarten and neither is the state of Maryland.

In fact, Agnew grew up in an environment that is a fine decompression chamber for anyone who may have been taught that politics is mainly concerned with two-party systems, the will of the majority and "may the best man win." Beneath the surface of the public issues bobbing between conservatives and liberals, segregationists and integrationists, tax-cutters and tax-spenders—and not very far beneath the surface—is the politics of money. For, as stated by the Federal Task Force Report on Organized Crime, describing the national scene in 1968, "The government is for sale . . . honesty is a pitfall. . . ."

Agnew entered politics with no money at all, and it takes money to run for office. Fortunately for him, he had no real opposition in the Republican primaries for county executive or for governor. The peculiarities of the general election campaigns for both these offices were such that he did not need a great deal of money, by current standards, to win. Still, he did require tens of thousands of dollars in the county race, and hundreds of thousands in the statewide race, and money in such amounts cannot be amassed from five- and ten-dollar contributions. It comes in large chunks from people who invest in government as they would in insurance or in stocks on the rise. And so, Agnew, who had never had any money, quickly came together with the big-money boys. Friends of his have a store of anecdotes illustrating his disdain for political dealing, especially in matters of money. But they also readily acknowledge his fascination with monied-men.

At first, having had no money, Agnew was perhaps tempted less; even the salary of a county executive, unadorned with other gratuities, would elevate him to an unaccustomed style of living. But as his dependency on the monied-men became an acknowledged thing; as he allowed himself to be courted and groomed by them; as he traveled with them, exchanged viewpoints with them, moved in their circles; he became less circumspect than his friends describe him as being in his earlier years. Perhaps he simply began to feel he belonged in that circle; that if it were proper to engage in politics with them, it also was proper to join them in business. But of course it was not proper to do so, and his business connections with the monied-men led to the only serious public charge about his ethics in office—his participation in the purchase of land along Chesapeake Bay. If that was his major indiscretion—or sole indiscretion—then he did, indeed, come through Maryland's political gauntlet remarkably unscathed.

It has already been pointed out that Agnew's term on the zoning board of appeals was free of any charges of skulduggery. Clarke Langrall, a Baltimore County insurance executive and a close friend, recalls that when Agnew was the appeals board chairman he once revealed to him the illicit financial gain that was inherent in his job. Langrall remembers Agnew telling him, "If I were interested, there is not a case that comes before me that I could not make a minimum of $10,000 on, under the table. You know that every one of these zoning appeals things run $50,000 to $100,000 difference in value of property. These cases amount to a hell of an amount of money." All types of business ventures were underway in the county, including large-scale land developments and investments of a growing magnitude. Agnew had apparently received some indirect overtures. "In a way it's tempting," he told Langrall, "But to me it's not at all tempting because it isn't worth it. I plan to go a lot further in life. To earn a quick dollar in that way isn't worth it at all." When the Democrats finally kicked Agnew off the board, the public squabble turned on the fact that Agnew had antagonized the Democratic county council by running for judge and by making public criticism of them. However, to Agnew's close friends, the reason appeared more nefarious. "Ted ran straight zoning," says Joe Pokorny, a former law partner, meaning that he would not "do business" with Democrats looking for zoning exceptions.

As he rose in politics, Agnew quickly learned that he had to "do business," at least to some degree and with some people. The root of the problem lay in raising money for campaigns. The sources of money for his two winning campaigns, for county executive and for governor, indelibly colored his administrations. Every hint of scandal that arose involved a person connected to his fund-raising activities.

In the campaign for county executive, the biggest donor was perhaps Albert Shuger, an apartment building developer and paint manufacturer. He not only raised money for Agnew but, at a critical point in the campaign, loaned him $4,000. Shuger had met Agnew through zoning board hearings. Later, in the interim period before his election as county executive, Shuger hired Agnew to represent him before the zoning board. After Agnew was elected, an accusation was made that Agnew had improperly tried to use his position as county executive to influence a zoning decision involving an apartment house at 7 Slade Avenue that belonged to Shuger.

The charge was made by Charles Steinbock, the Republican member of the zoning board named to replace Agnew after he had been removed. The two men had not been on good terms since then. At the time he made the charge, in 1966, Steinbock was perparing to enter the race for county executive, and the force of the charge was weakened by its political overtones and by the fact that he had waited nearly three years before making a public disclosure of the incident. Steinbock said that Agnew had asked him to grant Shuger a rezoning petition and that, later, one of Agnew's aides had asked him to allow the reclassification for the good of the Republican Party. The petition was denied by the board and its decision was later upheld by the Maryland Court of Appeals. "This infuriated Agnew, who is very easily infuriated," Steinbock recalls. Agnew's public reply was to accuse Steinbock of character assassination. "Those who know me know I don't do those things," Agnew said.

Campaign fund-raising was inevitably hazardous to the purity of one's reputation. For one thing, it was difficult to be discriminating as a Republican in a heavily Democratic county. Scott Moore, Agnew's chief fund-raiser in the campaign for county executive, managed to bring in about $10,000. (The entire campaign cost less than $35,000, according to Moore.) One of the things Moore did was to go to the courthouse and get lists of contributors to the Democratic party in the primary and the previous general election. Because of the rancor created by the Democratic primary fight and the victory of Mike Birmingham, the feeling was that Agnew might defeat the machine. Moore would confront contributors with the statements concerning their past donations to the Democratic party and say, "Now we want a contribution for our side." He collected a substantial amount of money this way. But these contributors were non-partisan givers, anxious only to buy into whoever was the victor. Moore also solicited architectural engineers and building contractors, a dangerous—but lucrative —source of money because of their dependence on government contracts. In fact, on election day, with an Agnew victory appearing imminent, one building contractor called Agnew headquarters before the ballots were even counted and said that he would pick up the tab for the entire campaign deficit. It was this type of contributor, men who were free with large sums of money, had obvious need for governmental favors, yet were careful to make no overt offers of deals, who proved to be the most difficult for Agnew to handle.

The contributors who came to him to trade directly, according to Clarke Langrall, got shut off completely. Langrall helped Agnew raise money in 1962 in the county, in 1966 in the state, and also for the national ticket in 1968. Of the 1966 campaign, Langrall says:

> One of the outstanding features of the $700,000 that we raised—a little short of that, $680,000 or $690,000— was rather unique in that Ted would not make any commitments to anybody, including me, the guy who chaired the committee. And to my knowledge, during the entire campaign [he] made not one single promise to anybody that he would, in fact, do this, that, or the other thing for them if he won.

Langrall recalls one person who offered $60,000 if Agnew would promise not to veto a certain bill if it passed the legislature. Agnew turned him down, even though the money, representing 10 per cent of the campaign total, was particularly needed at that time; $10,000 worth of obligations were pressing on him.

Langrall tells another story equally as interesting:

> When he was running for governor, a guy called and wanted to set up a dinner and have Ted appear. He'd guarantee $20,000 minimum; twenty contributors at $1,000 a head. I checked with Ted and he knew the guy and said "That's fine." It was going to be over in the Washington area. After it was all set and we were going to go—a few days before—the guy calls and says, "Are you coming along with the candidate?" and I said, "Yes, I'll be along." He said, "Anybody else?" and I said, "I don't know, you know how these things are," figuring the guy wanted to know how many places to set at the table. So I think it would be safe to say Ted, and somebody that will be driving him, and myself, so probably three of us. He said, "Well, I don't know how to approach this." I said, "What's the problem?" He said, "Would this person be Jewish?" I said, "I don't have any idea who it would be. He has people working with him that are Jewish. I don't know." He said, "Well, it's a difficult situation. Where we are having this dinner, this club frowns on us having Jewish guests." So I said, "I don't know what to tell you." He said, "Well, maybe you could arrange it so that the person wouldn't be Jewish." I said, "I couldn't do that but I'll mention it to Ted and see what he says." So I mentioned it to Ted. You know what he said? $20,000 minimum? "Fuck them. The hell with it." Now this is a campaign that was run nip and tuck. We always needed money. We never were even. And $20,000 at that point was just too much!
>
> I called the guy and told him, "Look, he isn't going to come." He said, "Well, look. You forget that. I'll take the responsibility." He backed off. And so Ted went. But this was very indicative of his character. He wasn't going for that.

Those lofty moments that Langrall recalls establish some of the boundaries of Agnew's conduct. But certainly he made deals and rewarded friends and supporters. And some of these rewards got him into trouble. Langrall himself figured in one episode.

Early in his administration in the county, Agnew had become concerned about the high cost of insurance, which was party attributable to the county's use of several insurance policies where a single one would suffice. In 1965, he announced that both the county government and the county board of education would seek a single life and health insurance plan for their 11,000 employees. The plan was to go before the county council for approval. Agnew ballyhooed it: "Never before in the history of our county has such a mutually beneficial program of such proportions been undertaken."

Sealed bids were solicited from sixty insurance firms. Two days later, a newspaper broke the story that Agnew had named three county insurance men, including Langrall, as "brokers of record" to deal with the insurance companies on the county's behalf and to share a brokers' fee which would be included in the insurance premium. The contract specifications carried no mention of the brokers. The entire incident was an example of very poor judgment; both the newspapers and the Democrats made the most of it. Agnew first blamed the flap on disgruntled insurance companies. "Yes, it's patronage," he said. "But bear in mind these are not just people picked to be recipients of political largesse. These are full-time insurance men." At one point, he told reporters, "If I had it to do all over again, I would never have appointed brokers of record. But to back off now would be tantamount to an admission of a lack of integrity and there is not impropriety here." Two days later, however, faced with an ultimatum from the Democratically controlled county council, he rescinded the appointments.

Jobs, liquor licenses, land purchases, building contracts—all these things fall under modern government patronage, legal or illegal, ethical or not, and Agnew at some time or other had to submit himself to the pressures of such decisions. Sometimes not even his closest staff members knew the process of resolution. For example, at one point during the gubernatorial campaign, Agnew casually told a few staff members that a man, whom Agnew did not name, had offered him a campaign contribution of $50,000, which he then upped to $75,000, if as governor, he would appoint a young relative of the man as a judge. No one heard any more, apparently, about this incident, so flippantly described by Agnew that day. Agnew is not a man to make promises under such circumstances, but he does believe in rewarding his friends. It is not known if the campaign contribution was finally accepted, but after Agnew became governor, a young relative of a prominent and wealthy man was named a judge.

During the same campaign, Robert Stofberg, a Baltimore businessman and backroom political arranger, told the press that he and Irvin Kovens, a business and political associate, were raising money for Agnew's campaign. Both Democrats, the men were partners in the Charlestown Race Track in West Virginia, and were known for their behind-the-scenes politicking. Kovens, for example, has been said to control appointments to a state regulatory agency Stofberg claims he and Kovens raised nearly $100,000 for Agnew in exchange for a promise that people they selected would be named to positions on regulatory agencies including the liquor board. Stofberg says the promise was kept.

Shortly after the election, the public learned through the press that Agnew, during the campaign, had had the services of Chick Lang, director of racing for Pimlico Race Track; Lang had been loaned out by the track owners, Ben and Herman Cohen. One reporter wrote, "The Cohens and Lang . . . backed a winner and their efforts could produce the biggest 'payoff' in Pimlico history." What Pimlico wanted, in its competition with other tracks in the state as well as in New York, New Jersey and West Virginia, was a more favorable schedule of racing dates. Agnew appointed Eldred Rinehart, a state Republican National Committeeman, as chairman of the state racing commission. Pimlico did not get its improved schedule, however. Instead the plum went to another Maryland race course, one that had retained the professional advice of George White, legal counsel to the Agnew campaign (and, in 1968, Agnew's vice-presidential campaign manager). The Cohens were enraged by what they regarded as double-dealing.

Some of Agnew's troubles over patronage were a result of the fact that he turned his back on fund-raising, as if by remaining personally ignorant of the money sources he could remove himself from any future taint. During his tenure as county executive he raised the issue of campaign contributions received by the Democrats from the pinball machine interests. The *Sun* papers' county reporters had been hammering at the subject for years. Stuart Smith, who was reporter for the *Sun* in Baltimore County when Agnew became county executive, had made it a personal campaign. (Before taking on the Baltimore County assignment, Smith had done an unending series of stories on the slot machines in other counties and had stirred enough interest to force the legislature to outlaw them.) Agnew's anti-pinball attitude was, in fact, an early attempt to win Smith's confidence; his aides agree that he had more respect for Smith as a reporter than for any other newsman. Later, the *Sun* assigned Ben Orrick to the county. Orrick continued the attack on the pinball promoters and, with one series of stories, got the chairman of the county liquor board, Roland Volz, removed because of an allegation of conflict of interest. Agnew's attack on the pinball machine distributors, therefore, was nothing new or different. What was different, however, was the rebuttal of the Democrats, who claimed that Agnew himself had had pinball money behind him in his campaign for county executive in 1962. The Democrats pushed Agnew to the wall on the issue and he came out looking badly.

Reconstructed now, it appears that Agnew did not know he had received that support. Dale Anderson, the man who challenged Agnew on the issue and now Baltimore County executive himself, believes Agnew was not directly involved in collecting the money. Anderson has affidavits, which he showed to the press at the time, in which various pinball machine distributors swore they donated money to Agnew's campaign in 1962 and to the Republicans in an interim election in 1964. But none of the affidavits name Agnew as the direct recipient. Apparently, the money was collected by Scott Moore; the Moore family had a long-standing friendship with Roland Volz whose Rossville Vending Corporation controlled the pinballs. Anderson produced the affidavits when he and Moore were opposing each other for the office of county executive and Agnew was running for governor. He claims now that the newspaper and television newsmen photographed them but never used them because they did not want to harm Agnew's chances of stopping George Mahoney. Agnew's response was to bluff. Probably by then he learned that he had, in fact, been the recipient of pinball money. He told Anderson to take the affidavits to the grand jury. Anderson replied in a letter that since the affidavits involved Agnew's people, not Democrats, Agnew ought to go before the grand jury, and he offered Agnew the affidavits. There, the matter lapsed, since the Democrats were too involved to pursue it further.

In 1966, Agnew himself charged that he had been offered $200,000 by Maryland slot machine interests if he would promise not to veto legislation extending the life of these gambling devices in southern Maryland. The machines had been outlawed (after Smith's crusade) in all but four counties, where they played an important part in the economy. Each year the question of their continuance came up before the legislature in the midst of heavy lobbying. Agnew claimed he had been approached three times during the campaign with offers of $20,000, then $75,000, and finally $200,000. Three of the Democratic candidates acknowledged that they also had been approached on the subject, but said that no specific offers had been made. The Baltimore County state's attorney, a Democrat, pointed out that the offer described by Agnew constituted an attempted bribe and that Agnew had a public duty to report the facts and identify those who had offered the bribe. Agnew refused to do so and, as in the pinball matter, the issue died out when Agnew withdrew. In both cases, he apparently thought he was on firm ground, and could demonstrate that he was free of the taint of organized gambling interests. In both cases he got caught in his own loose charges.

To the discomfort of many of his political friends, Agnew got caught up in the sphere of influence of several of the Baltimore county monied-men as soon as he became county executive. These were men who chose to become intimate with the holders of political power in the county regardless of party or personality. They constituted a circle of acquaintances different from old political friends: Scott Moore, his brother Dutch Moore, Clarke Langrall, or the few social friends, known as the Gang, who made up a Saturday night group of husbands and

wives. The monied-men were set apart in a world of their own—
some were county bluebloods, others Jews, some businessmen,
others bankers—but all of them lived on a loftier, more rarefied
financial plane than any of Agnew's other acquaintances or
Agnew himself.

Joe Pokorny, Agnew's former law partner, describes them
like this:

> . . . These people you're talking about are a breed apart
> from average-Joe citizens. These are the doers, these are
> the contributors . . . these are the people that are building
> the big office complexes, the big shopping store complexes;
> you need it or you can't go shopping. So. They need it.
> Now the question is, how to get them? They're needed,
> they fit in as part of the planning; they fit in as part of
> the *big* planning. They have the money to do this.

These people, who are "a breed apart" to Pokorny, are the
same ones whom C. Wright Mills called "The Very Rich."
In *The Power Elite*, Mills identified them in a way that all of
Agnew's friends would recognize and understand:

> The major economic fact about the very rich is the fact
> of the accumulation of advantages: those who have great
> wealth are in a dozen strategic positions to make it yield
> further wealth.

Not only did Agnew's closest political friends (who were
not "the very rich") understand Mills' insight, they feared
its implication. Because in suburban America since World
War II, the "major economic fact" quite possibly has been the
intimate relationship between the politician and "the very
rich," the apartment and housing and land developers and
those who are connected with them, the banks, savings and loan
corporations, builders, contractors, etc. When Agnew decided to
give his total support to urban renewal in Baltimore County,
Dutch Moore, fearful of Agnew's naïveté, got so nervous he
started his own private inquiry into the plan. "I thought that
[there] was some fantastic real estate swindle involved in urban
renewal. I just saw it. I couldn't see anything else." Obviously
urban renewal, offering property for private development, was
a golden opportunity for the very rich. Moore worried about

those around Agnew who had one hand on the county executive's back, while the other hand was counting up their assets. He eventually was convinced that the plan was safeguarded and so open that there was little room for real thievery.

> Now there could have been hanky-panky on one or two properties . . . there are always ways of doing this . . . but as far as there being any major swindles or real estate transactions that would hurt the plan or embarrass anybody, there was no chance of this. I'm absolutely convinced of this. . . . It was just too open a plan.

The problem, in the minds of some of Agnew's associates, was Agnew himself. There was patronage being handed out, favors to friends, and Agnew's sense of loyalty toward his supporters. That was one thing. But he was naïve, they believed, when it came to dealing with the very rich. "In my opinion," says Sam Kimmel, an early friend and law partner, "I think [Agnew] places too much confidence in these people, in their integrity, or in their determination not to get him in trouble. I think he is not careful enough."

Dutch Moore's nervousness over urban renewal partly stemmed from his contact with the very rich who were operating in and out of Agnew's office. Through his brother Scott, Dutch Moore came to Agnew as an aide with no official title, but he soon developed into one of Agnew's principal staff members, becoming executive assistant, in effect, office manager. All the paperwork moving to and from Agnew's desk passed through Dutch Moore's hands, as well as all correspondence that was channeled away from Agnew himself to be handled routinely by other staff members or agency heads. In addition, Dutch Moore, because of his wide political contacts, handled many political problems for Agnew. Eventually, he became responsible for all patronage; Agnew quickly grew bored with this aspect of his office. And Moore remembers clearly the intrusions of the very rich. For example, there is one man who will here be called Mathews:

> I can remember one instance in my office in the county when [Mathews] came in and indicated to Al Kaltenbach,

who was the director of public works, that Ted had approved such and such a project that he [Mathews] was
interested in, and to get the thing going. And Al came
up to see me and said, "I have just gotten it from
[Mathews] who has just seen Ted and this thing is supposed to get off the ground." . . . I knew for a fact that this
wasn't so; that Ted was absolutely opposed to it; that
[Mathews] hadn't seen Ted that day, and that what he'd
done was just gone to Kaitenbach and told him, "I've
talked this over with Ted and he wants me to get it going
for him, wants me to handle it for him." . . . And he was
close enough to [Agnew] that these fellows would believe
him.

Moore remembers another case involving Mathews which
occurred while Agnew was governor. The state was interested
in finding a site for a regional office building center in the
suburbs outside of the District of Columbia, either in Montgomery or Prince Georges counties. Mathews and a friend
owned a piece of suitably located property which Mathews sub-
mitted informally to the board of public works for approval.
The impression was that Agnew favored it. Moore recalls that
the "proposition" eventually worked back to his desk; until
then he hadn't heard anything about it. And when he ex-
amined the proposal, for a building to be erected and leased
to the state, he found that it called for a rental that was about
one dollar a square foot over the market price.
Moore recalls:

I picked up the phone and called Ted and said, "Look,
there seems to be a lot of pressure on this project and
it seems to be coming from you. It's out of line. Do you
want me to do some more work on it, or do you want
me to knock it in the head?" He said, "Dutch, my position
is the same now as it's always been. If I can help my
friends I'm going to help them, but only if it's in line
with what anybody else can do." And I think this was
always his attitude. If he could help a friend and it was
on the basis of everybody else's bid being the same, he
wanted the friend to get it. If the bid were higher from

the friend, that's tough. And I've never seen Ted make
an exception to this type of thing.

Moore and others felt there was a strong need to watch out
for Agnew, to prevent him from the compromising entangle-
ments that he always seemed about to get tied up in. As county
executive, on a trip back from San Diego, Agnew, at the insistent invitation of Irvin Kovens, the Baltimore Democratic
political power, and presence in many regulatory areas, stopped
over at Las Vegas, staying at Caesar's Palace, a gambling casino
and hotel owned by a Baltimore combine. Agnew was furious
when he was accused of accepting accommodations from Kovens
and he denied it. But while he was running with Nixon in the
1968 campaign, apparently having learned no lesson, he had to
be stopped by an aide from checking into a casino on an overnight stay in Las Vegas. The aide arranged accommodations for
him outside the city's sin strip.

There is in Agnew no understanding of the necessity for a
façade of propriety in addition to proper behavior itself. Agnew apparently credits himself with some "high morality"
which he feels to be in itself sufficient answer to any suspicions
of dubious conduct. ("Those who know me know I don't do
those things," as he told the public in the 7 Slade Avenue
zoning dispute.) Confronted with charges built on his actions
or statements, he rebuts with references to his private motivations. When he was upbraided for labeling Hubert Humphrey
"squishy soft on communism," he denied that he was trying
to resurrect old and dangerous political passions; when he
called Gene Oishi of the *Sun* "fat Jap," he refused to apologize to him because he expected Oishi to understand that no
insult was intended. "It is very inconvenient," Agnew said,
referring to the "squishy soft" remark, "for candidates to have
their fluency burdened by having to stop and think every time
they put a few words together." And so, neither his words, nor
his actions are to be taken as indicators of the true inner man.
It is a position out of *Alice in Wonderland*, certainly not the
kind of blanket exemption from responsibility that Agnew
would grant to others, political opponents or otherwise. As a
lawyer, he surely must understand that no real defense can be

made in a case in which everything, absolutely everything, must rest on character witnesses, especially the defendant's own self-appraisal of his character (". . . I don't do these things"). Yet that is just what he asks of the public.

Given his naïveté in these matters, it was fortunate for Agnew that such incidents as those involving the pinball money were mere ripples that were smoothed away and forgotten. One incident that did not die, however, was his land purchase on Chesapeake Bay. The purchase apparently was made in June 1965; Agnew voluntarily revealed it on July 6, 1966, during his gubernatorial campaign. On July 8 he announced he would divest himself of his interest in the property and public concern about the matter died. However, on October 22, 1968, during the presidential campaign, the New York *Times* ran a detailed account of the transaction and concluded that Agnew had been guilty of conflict of interest which indicated his unfitness to serve as Vice President.

The property consisted of 107 acres in Anne Arundel County near the present Chesapeake Bay Bridge. Six months after the purchase Governor Millard Tawes introduced plans for a second bay bridge to run parallel with the first. Those plans ran into great difficulty as a controversy arose over the need for a second span and the question as to whether a second bridge might be more suitable farther to the north, near the Baltimore metropolitan area, or farther south, where it could serve the Washington metropolitan area. Tawes steadfastly remained fixed on a parallel span, even in the face of a public referendum which rejected the idea. Tawes was constitutionally forbidden to run for re-election in 1966; when Agnew entered the race, the matter of the bay bridge was still in the air and would be a problem facing the new governor. It was this that prompted Agnew to disclose his land interest. His opponents immediately demanded that Agnew either sell his interest or withdraw from the race. Agnew announced he would sell and denied all political implications in the transactions. He said there had been no attempt to conceal the purchase, the land records were open to the public and his name was first on the deeds. The county executive of Baltimore County had no authority over the selection of land for a state bridge in Anne Arundel County. "I feel that this disclosure was complete and timely," said Agnew. "I don't expect you to believe it but when this transaction was being worked out, not one of us said anything about the parallel bridge. It didn't occur to us." Later he said, "This transaction was above reproach."

Aside from the possible conflict of interest, the most disquieting aspect of the matter was the other names listed as members of the combine owning the land; those names would have cast serious reflection on Agnew even if the deal involved only a hot dog stand in the Adirondacks. The real question, one which escaped Agnew's sensibilities entirely, was the propriety of *any* business deal joining the Baltimore county executive and the other eight men, among whom were J. Walter Jones, Harry A. Dundore, Leonard O. Gerber, and Lester Matz. The name that probably raised the greatest local interest was that of J. Walter Jones.

Jones was a real estate speculator, and was on the board of the Chesapeake National Bank. He had frequently appeared before Agnew as an expert witness at zoning appeals board hearings. He was a Democrat, but in the words of one Agnew associate, "Walter has a way of being very close to key men at key times—and later on doesn't know them." Jones was "very close" to Christian Kahl and one of his supporters during the Democratic primary when Kahl opposed Birmingham for the county executive nomination. After Kahl lost the primary and Agnew won the general election, Jones became "very close" to Agnew. So close, in fact, that Agnew often consulted him on governmental matters to the exclusion of others in government or on his staff. Agnew liked him, admired him and, in the words of some of his friends, "was in awe of Walter." J. Walter Jones became, and remains, the closest to Agnew of the very rich. According to one newspaper account, in the two years preceding the disclosure of the bay bridge land purchase, J. Walter Jones had received $24,135 for appraisal services for Baltimore County, then under the Agnew administration. Another man on the list, Lester Matz, was a partner in the engineering firm of Matz, Childs and Associates, a firm that received $315,061 for county work during the Agnew administration.

Agnew's participation in a business deal with these men was a blatant affront to public interest. The facts of modern day political corruption could lead the public to no other conclusion than that Agnew's inclusion in the deal was a payoff. Whether *in fact* it was a payoff becomes irrelevant. The sophisticated payoffs in contemporary usage involve the transfer of land. An official is allowed to purchase a piece of property at a price which is either far below the real value, or else he is sold property which, for some foreseeable reason, vastly increases in price in a short time. This kind of deal is widely known to be practiced in Maryland. But it is a safe kind of corruption. Even if such deals are exposed and the actual participants are named in deeds, it is almost impossible to fill in all the links necessary to building a case strong enough to bring before a grand jury, or even, indeed, strong enough to make an unimpeachable case before the public.

It can only be wondered how Agnew could have believed that the act of participation in a private business deal with men already fulfilling county contracts could be considered "above reproach." A parallel he might understand are the various grounds for mistrials when a witness or a lawyer in a case converses with a member of the jury outside of court, even if the conversation deals only with the weather or where the men's room is located. The issue of the bay bridge land has become a bore to most people in Maryland who have heard all the facts before and lived through its resurrection by the New York *Times* in 1968. But it remains pertinent because it bears so importantly on Agnew's view of his character as unimpeachable and his judgment as infallible, two immunities from human frailty that he, like many others in political life, seems to think come with elective office.

Behind the facts of the Chesapeake Bay business venture are a host of unanswered questions. Why had Agnew been invited into the deal? What was his major contribution, money or influence? Did *any* of the partners have prior knowledge of the plans for a parallel bridge? Why would Agnew invest in what would be a speculative deal of little promise if no inside information were available to the partners? Where did Agnew get the money for the venture? If it was loaned to him, why would a loan be available to him for such a seemingly unprofitable undertaking? Was it, in fact, good for the deal to include the Baltimore County Executive? Was it, in fact, potentially profitable for a Baltimore County Executive to enter into such a deal? And on, and on.

Dutch Moore has an unshakable belief in Agnew's honesty, but serious doubts about his financial acumen. "He's almost like a child," Moore says. "He doesn't realize what money is. He makes some crazy investments. . . . And the biggest and worst investment he could have made was the piece of ground on the bay bridge approach that they bought. Not from the standpoint that he could have gotten hurt. It just wasn't that good of an investment for the risk he took in going to a venture of that type and the type of people he went into it with." And this raises the final question. Assuming no one in the partnership had any knowledge of the plans for a second bridge, and that the investment was a poor one that Agnew was too naïve to realize, then how to account for such sharp and successful business entrepreneurs as Jones, Dondore, etc., entering into such a deal?

Agnew's involvement in the bay bridge deal symbolizes how far he had come, in terms of material success, since his entry into politics. As recently as 1962, when he was running for county executive, his partner Ed Hardesty had found him sitting at his desk sunk in depression about his finances and the crushing debts he had incurred. But by 1963, along with J. Walter Jones, he was a member of the board of directors of the Chesapeake National Bank. And by 1965 he was a partner in the bay bridge land deal. And by 1966 when he campaigned for governor, he could declare his net worth at $100,000. In less than three years he moved forward from the starting line in the race toward the American Dream to a point where he found himself, to use C. Wright Mills' words, "in a dozen strategic positions" to make his money make more money.

When Agnew sold his bay bridge property, it was not because he personally was troubled by any questions of impropriety; and obviously he had learned no lessons. As was discovered later, he had also invested in a condominium in the Virgin Islands. His partners in that transaction were, and still are, most of those he had joined in the bay bridge deal, with the addition of the county executive of Anne Arundel County (where the bay bridge property was located) and other Anne Arundel County public officials. On that, Dutch Moore says:

. . . I was offered a piece of that thing. If I had a lot of money and wanted to travel to the Virgin Islands and write it off as a tax trip, fine. But that was the only damage I could see. If you look into that . . . the boys set that up to accommodate some political friends, that's all. No great money-making venture there. In fact, I doubt, considering the money Ted put in it, they probably had to borrow the money. I suspect it's a loser.

Perhaps it is a loser, or will be. But to have reached the point of being able to take a tax write-off on a losing venture of even that magnitude might well have seemed like the pinnacle of success to the Spiro Agnew of only a very few years earlier. He was involved in business with the very rich. And his political career had only begun.

14 AGNEW HAS A love-hate relationship with the press—probably because he was spoiled when he was young. For although the relationship is unacknowledged on both sides, the political Agnew is the love child of the liberal press, specifically of the *Sun* papers of Baltimore. The *Sun* papers have never been promiscuous in their search for good government, but an alliance with this cause resulted in the political Agnew. Now, as Vice President, he has become the liberal press's problem child—irascible, uncontrollable, disrespectful of his elders, unable to take advice, disobedient and ungrateful to his parents. Agnew himself has singled out two root causes of our national discontent: permissiveness (of parents and of society in general) and masochistic self-guilt, the natural result, in Agnew's view, is the misbehavior of student and civil rights demonstrators and ghetto rioters. Agnew's actions in relation to the press fall precisely into this same pattern, for what element of American society is more permissive or more self-guilty than the press? "None of these people wanted anything but the best," said Agnew in a speech "yet they have reaped the worst."

The nation accepts Agnew's statements on the press at face value as the thinking of a critic, or a disgruntled politician, or at worst, a right-winger intent on repealing the First Amendment. But that is because attention is on his words and his words are no clue to the motive for his attack in the first place. The press has its serious critics. It is sensitive, self-conscious, and agonizingly self-critical, even as it is quick to rise in self-defense against outside snipers. Agnew has not contributed to that serious discourse. It does not suit his purpose to do so. It is far more profitable to string together some loosely related quotes to demonstrate how anti-Nixon, anti-Agnew or anti-

American the press and its spokesmen are. Agnew's attacks draw also from a well-stocked library of criticism which the far right has circulated for years; its targets are his—the Washington *Post,* the New York *Times, Newsweek,* and Averell Harriman, who always seems to get squeezed in, even though he lacks press credentials. These right-wing fetishes may well stem from his speech writers, whose typewriters seem to have built into them copies of "A Choice Not an Echo" and "None Dare Call It Treason," those popular far-right tracts that detail just how bad the liberal press has been.

But the interesting aspect of Agnew's relationship with the press does not lie in the simplistic content of his speeches against it. It is not the what but the why that is revealing.

The press was both mother and father to Agnew the politician. He was wanted and needed before he arrived. And when he arrived, the press nourished him and protected him, encouraged and counseled him, scolded him when he deserved it, praised him when he earned praise and, sometimes, only when he needed encouragement. Above all, the press truly wanted to love him and disowned him only when he disowned the press. On his part, Agnew never was comfortable with the relationship. He never understood it, not his role, not the role of the press. There was constant bickering, hurt feelings and disappointment. He was resentful of criticism and much too taken with praise. He wanted the press to be even more permissive than it was, at least so far as he was concerned. As for the press itself, they too were let down, for Agnew did not turn out to be the son they hoped he would be. Such a child can feel guilty and find it hard to apologize or express gratitude. Permissiveness breeds rebellion, anyway, Agnew says. And he now attacks the press for the same reason that an unruly child misbehaves to attract attention. Even a spanking is better than being ignored.

* * *

Agnew got his first taste of publicity by working up the ladder of civic organizations to become president of the Kiwanis Club and president of the county Parent-Teacher Association. He could see, as all young lawyers do, the value of such exposure to his law career and to any future interest in politics. Psychologically, he seems to have been one whose constitution could not tolerate casual experimentation. The very first sniff, the first drag, the first speedball in the form of a headline, or shot in the arm in the form of a picture, addicted him. He is more than fascinated by publicity, he is hooked on it. Now he is mainlining a three-a-day habit—with the morning press, the afternoon press and the evening television. But at first the highs were few and hard to come by.

Agnew began to take publicity seriously when he went on the zoning appeals board. At that time he told a friend that the press was extremely important to a politician in a minority party; he began to discover that strong words, catchy phrases, name-calling and political infighting were the elements that captured space and headlines. Certainly strong language and aggressiveness are natural to him, but he deliberately began to play the press and to gather publicity as one would a cash crop. It was not valuable enough to win him a seat on the court when he ran for that position, but the number of votes he won convinced him that he was on the right course. From 1958 through 1961 every elective office in the county was held by a Democrat. Agnew, the appointed minority member of the appeals board, was the closest thing to a public official that the Republican party had. And the publicity he received when he was removed from that board, as we have seen, convinced him he could capture an elective office. From that time on to the present there has been rarely a time when Spiro Agnew was not thrusting himself onto the pages of newspapers and the screens of television sets on a local, statewide, or national scale.

His campaign to become county executive was designed around his analysis of the local press, specifically the *Sun* papers, a locally owned morning and afternoon daily combination. Neither the *Evening Sun* nor the *Sun* (the morning paper) had as large a circulation as the *News-American* (which was then the *News-Post*), a Hearst-owned paper, but the editorial influence of the *Sun* papers was far greater, as was the prestige of its reporting.

Since Agnew's opponent, Mike Birmingham, was boss of the Democratic machine, it was a foregone conclusion that the three dailies would endorse Agnew—they had been attacking the machine for years. To ensure that endorsement, Agnew devised a platform to appeal specifically to the newspapers. It included some ideas for improving the tax situation and industrial development and it supported public accommodations legislation to eliminate racial segregation in public places. This last issue was already before the state legislature, but to bring it to life in the local county campaign Agnew persuaded a maverick Democrat on the county council to introduce a measure before that body. Birmingham escaped the issue to his own satisfaction by pointing out that in four months the General Assembly would act on a state bill which would have preference over local legislation. Agnew nevertheless promised to make an issue of racial bias in public places and went ahead with it, not so much running against Birmingham as running with the newspapers. Finally, to lock up the support of the *Sun* papers' county reporters and the editorial writers themselves, Agnew pledged himself to outlaw pinball machines in the county. The *Sun* had been plugging away at that issue also, convinced that the pinballs were bankrolling the Democratic machine and were a major source of political corruption. Dutch Moore recalled in an interview Agnew's concern with pinball machines:

"One of those things that Ted early in the game picked up was the fact that the *Sun* papers' editorial staff would write an editorial on pinballs on every day in the week if he could just give them some excuse."

Edgar Jones, an editorial writer on the *Sun* who specialized in local issues, also recalled that early race:

> . . . when he [Agnew] was running for county executive he was running as a reform candidate and certainly we were important to him. We had been critical of the previous administration. . . . In fact, we had been critical of the administration out there for, I suppose, a decade. In a sense, he needed us and we needed him. We needed someone who would be a reform candidate. So that . . . I suppose he felt close to us and to some extent we felt close to him. It wasn't on the basis of friendship, that is, I don't know of anybody who looked on him as a friend, who knew him, other than his political life.

When Agnew won that election, the *Sun* papers and the county felt they had a reform executive at last; Republicans felt they had the start of a real party organization; liberals and Negroes felt they had some liberal leadership. None of this was true.

Agnew's term as county executive amounted to one long public relations campaign. These were Agnew's early, permissive years with the press, when the newspapers were sustaining and supportive. Yet the relationship was not quite the simple one recalled by Edgar Jones. It was true that the press needed someone who would be a reform candidate, and Agnew certainly needed press exposure. But he did not view the relationship as a mutual pact for the common good. He felt, rather, that he was on to something, that he could outsmart the press and use it for his own ends. Thinking, or at least hoping, that they had the kind of public official they had been looking for over the past decade, the press was happy to be manipulated, hoping that the result would be good government. But for Agnew, with the press responding so willingly to his manipulation, there grew up an expectancy that things would always be that way.

Agnew entered office on a wave of support from the press which continued undiminished in strength for a time. He made some sound appointments to key positions on his personal staff—Scott Moore, for example, his brother Dutch Moore, and others. He retained in office several Democrats who headed key bureaus, thus establishing a bipartisanship that was widely approved and brought him the praise of county weekly newspapers that were oriented to the Democratic party.

The press was so anxious to approve that they misread Agnew's motivations, giving him credit where none was due. One case of this kind involved a maneuver in Agnew's continuing feud with J. Fife Symington. Following Agnew's election, one of Symington's supporters, a loyal Republican organization man, boasted that he was to receive the patronage business of trash-collecting in the Essex area of the county. Agnew heard of this and issued a statement denouncing the rumor and the practice of making a vital public service into a political deal. This public rebuke let Symington know that it would be Agnew, and not the party's central committee, who would distribute patronage. Party leaders were furious but the press applauded the statement as an indication that Agnew's administration would be above what had become "politics-as-usual" in previous administrations.

Agnew hired into his administration several newsmen, a practice not uncommon in Maryland or elsewhere, but Agnew did so with the personal sense of having "bought" a knowledgable person away from his position as a potentially troublesome outside critic. He began probing the working reporters to determine what kinds of relationships he could establish with them. The newspaper reporters concerned him more than those from the television and radio stations. Television reporters normally would ask him a prearranged question and pull back to allow the cameras to film what he had to say. Or they would ask him to read a portion of a statement into the cameras. The possibilities of television as a medium of publicity—propaganda, actually—excited him. But it was the printed press that put him in awe. Newspaper reporters worked up a story, filled in background, sought out other sources and opinions. He had less control over his statements in print than he had on television. There was no way of knowing in what context a news release would appear in the newspapers. And so he courted the print reporters seriously, called them in for chats, tried out ideas on them, and attempted to learn in advance what the press reactions to his moves would be. What he wanted was as much publicity as he could get—and absolutely no public criticism.

"He took the position . . . as far as the use of television, that it was the best free advertisement he could possibly get," said Scott Moore. "And the same thing with the press; and that he should use it and that that should come first, at all times, because it was free. You didn't have to pay for it, and it covered the waterfront—it covered all the people of the county.

"He said you could always wait until the last months prior to an election and pay for the television, pay for the radio and you couldn't get anywhere near the amount of coverage that you would if you just worked at it full time, all the time. And he did work at it. There was never, in my judgment, a reporter or television cameraman or somebody—if they wanted to see Agnew, he was there, he was ready to speak."

Agnew made a little discovery that he parlayed into a full-fledged technique. He noticed that whenever a television reporter and cameraman came to him and taped anything, at least some part of it invariably appeared on the screen. This was not true of a newspaper reporter's interview, which might or might not lead to a story. But television crews, lugging their heavy equipment or hauling it on hand trucks, always had some result of their labor on the suppertime news shows. This lead him to realize that all he needed to do to get on the evening screen was to create a pretext for getting the cameras to him. And so he instituted regular press conferences, to guarantee his periodic appearance in area living rooms, regardless of what real news his administration was making.

Agnew's tall, straight, superbly attired figure was ideal for television. His command of facts and figures was impressive. His willingness to continue a controversy or create a new one made him an interesting gamble on even a dull news day. And his speech style was as vitriolic then as it is now. Everything was made as convenient as possible for the press. The newsroom in the Baltimore County office building was on the third floor, just down the corridor from Agnew's office. Very often he would deliver press releases himself and then stay on in the newsroom for additional questions from the reporters. He would call the radio stations and read his statements over the phone for broadcast recordings. One suspects that Agnew's fateful meeting with the black leaders in 1968 was held in Baltimore, rather than at the capitol in Annapolis, to make certain that no reporters would miss it because of the inconvenience of traveling to Annapolis.

The consideration Agnew extended to the press was also designed to win the favor of reporters. And it tells something about Agnew's cynicism that he always regarded favorable stories as having been the result of his solicitousness rather than honest, independent appraisals by the newsmen. In the course of one running feud between Agnew and a county councilman, the *Sun*'s county reporter Ben Orrick would contact either Agnew or Scott Moore each time the councilman let go a new salvo directed at Agnew. Both Agnew and Moore believed that Orrick was favoring them with the tips so that Agnew could balance the attack with his own rebuttal. It would not fit their view of the press to believe that in all such controversies a *Sun* reporter would attempt to wrap up both sides of the story simultaneously if he could. And yet the relationship between Orrick and Agnew was not one of trust, but of mutual wariness. On more than one occasion, particularly when Orrick was asking pointed questions about irregularities in Agnew's administration, Agnew reacted with fury and ordered the newsman out of his office.

Agnew also began the practice of meeting for lunch with editorial writers from the *Sun* papers and the Baltimore *News-Post*. This practice is not uncommon and can be mutually beneficial to both parties, giving the writers a chance to get some first-hand understanding of administration policy, which, in itself, is beneficial to the politician whose actions are scrutinized in editorials. But Agnew had his private view of the relationship of the press to his administration. They had supported his candidacy and applauded his election. He looked on the papers as his supporters, no different in kind than any others, and he seemed to expect unwavering loyalty, rather than a re-examination on each issue that came along. What was accomplished by those luncheons was viewed in completely different lights in the county office building and on Calvert Street in downtown Baltimore, where the *Sun* is located.

In an interview, Edgar Jones of the *Sun* (morning) discussed Agnew's lunches:

> Sometime, it must have been when he was county executive that he inquired around and found that I did most of the local editorials and that my field was local government. . . . What he did, he used to invite Dudley Digges [editorial writer on the *Evening Sun*] and myself to lunch, not regularly, but three or four times a year, maybe a little more often than that, to discuss things.
>
> . . . I think he very much wanted to know ahead of time and feel assured that the papers would go along with him [on pending issues and policies]. . . . That's what the purpose of these luncheons and things were, really, and I think he would have loved to have been able to get that kind of a commitment or even a sort of positive feeling from Dudley Digges and myself that, you know, that we would support this and would look upon it favorably.
>
> We couldn't do that, except in a general sort of way,

but after all, when you're dealing with two editorial writers—you know, we get involved in an editorial conference every morning and it's one person's opinion against another so it wouldn't have been possible for us to make any commitment, anyway. But he liked to sound us out. That certainly was the purpose of this.

This is how Dutch Moore, Agnew's administrative assistant, recalls those meetings:

You know he worked very hard to establish a good press relationship and met with the editors of the *News-Post* and the *Sun* periodically, maybe every two weeks he had lunch with them. . . . He frequently would try things out on them to see what their reactions would be. In fact, he'd try something new on them just to see what their impression might be, how they were going to handle it editorially, maybe, to see whether they would support it.

I think if he saw that they were totally against it, he would drop it immediately. If he saw that they had no real faults about it one way or the other, he'd act, depending upon how important he thought it may be to the county. And if they were really in favor of it, regardless of how good it was or important it was, he'd push the thing just because he could get a favorable editorial some time along the line when he wanted one.

And here is how Scott Moore, Agnew's county solicitor and his closest political friend, saw it:

The relationship with the media . . . I thought was just unbelievable . . . In the way he managed them. I think it is so ironic, looking back, the way the newspapers have turned against him, particularly the ones he had eating out of his hands for years, and I am talking about specifically, the *Sun* papers.

. . . Ted got to know the editors of the *Sun* papers and got to know them very well, and before he made any major decision he'd call up some of these editors and discuss it with them, and when he made a decision they would invariably write a very, very flattering editorial. I shook my head.

The only thing that frightens me, suppose somebody who really has an ax to grind and was out to, I mean, who was a little dictator or something, was able to do this same thing and manage the news the way Agnew did it.

I'm not saying that there was anything really improper about it, but he would kind of use them in some respects. He would want to find out if it was a good political position to be in, and he knew if they liked it and they were consulted first—and they like the idea of being consulted by a county executive, that there would be good editorials to follow. And, brother, the proof is in the pudding! Just look at the editorials about Agnew in the period of four years that he was in there. They just didn't happen in any way, shape or form. He fostered it—he put the bait out there and they took it.

One aide recalls that Agnew threw himself into the issue of taxes after returning from a luncheon during which Edgar Jones had told him to "make a splash" about taxes. Shortly after he took office, Agnew learned of the editorial interest in urban renewal. "Make it our program," he told his staff, "the *Sun* papers will eat it up."

And so Agnew received the encouragement and support of the *Sun* papers. The *Sun* papers felt they were helping a reform candidate in whom they had placed great hope, but this help was viewed by Agnew and those around him as having been won by Agnew's artful tactics.

Agnew's day-to-day relationship with the reporters, on the other hand, soured for him rather quickly. Generally, they were easy on him. "My God, compared to the others out there in the county, he looked great. You had to believe he was the best and the most honest administrator. Look at who else you had to deal with out there?" Ben Orrick says now. But when some issues arose dealing with the integrity of Agnew's administration, the reporters hit him hard and Agnew was both angry and perplexed. To him, the reporters were employees of organizations that had supported him politically and hence adverse stories were out of line. He would attempt to stop such stories ahead of time, or get them toned down, by calling the editors of the newspapers. Edgar Jones was the recipient of many of those calls. To him they indicated Agnew's continuing inability to understand the press, its role in society, its relation to government and such internal policies as the freedom granted to reporters.

> . . . His view of the press was never the same as mine. He had, and still does, I think, a feeling that it was the function of the press to support the good guys. And if the good guys are in government, to support the government at whatever level.
>
> So that I used to get a number of calls at home from him, because he was so distressed by news stories. His general feeling was, "Why is the *Sun* printing these stories? They're for me; they want to see me become governor, so why do they print these stories?" Well, from our point of view, you print news because it's news . . . whether its owning land where the parallel bay bridge is going or whether it is apartment zoning—what was that, 11 Slade Avenue?—there were a couple of other stories.
>
> I think he really felt that it was the function of newspapers, and in particular, the function of the *Sun,* to help his government in every way possible, and as far as possible, not to say things which detracted from him.
>
> I think that he really considered himself right, and pretty much above reproach, and if someone were going to charge him with something like the Slade Avenue thing, that the reporter—because I have had calls where he complained to me about reporters and news people—that they should have come to him and printed his full statement and all at the same time and put the whole thing in a better light. I don't think he really expected us not to print some of these things. He just thought we should be doing the whole thing in a way that would put him in a better light.
>
> I can't remember whether it was the Slade Avenue thing . . . where he called me at home and wanted a reporter to stop—stop what the reporter was doing. It was Ben Orrick, I think, who was a good man, and a county resident and all that.
>
> I would have explained to him that the editorial de-

partment has simply no connection with the news department—no control. We don't want them to tell us how to write editorials and they don't want us to tell them how to write news stories. It was another aspect of newspapers that I think he never understood. He felt that if the editorial department was supporting him, then it was up to the editorial department to go out and tell Ben Orrick not to write any more about Slade Avenue.

. . . he feels about the press, that the press, in effect, chooses up sides and that the sides should be helping the government, and [now], I think, helping the Nixon administration. In this case, he is part of the Nixon administration and the Nixon administration is trying to do good things. Therefore, the press should be helping *and not criticizing.*

Whe he couldn't get satisfaction from reporters or editorial writers, and sometimes even when he did, Agnew turned to the device of writing letters to the editor. The letters were frequent and lengthy and often turned on picayune points. But they were printed. That counted.

As time went on during his county administration, Agnew grew more, not less, concerned with the press. He paid attention to the details of news coverage. He would ask television reporters and cameramen for their opinions on his presentation and technique before the cameras. He listened to their advice carefully and mastered the medium with the help of their friendly criticism. Dutch Moore particularly recalls Agnew's concerns with the language of stories that appeared about him:

Ted invariably will look at every single sentence and every single word and any particular thing that interests him, and it's amazing the way he can pick out one little word or one little sentence as far as how it affects him, or what his feeling is with reference to this particular sentence . . . many a time we'd say "Don't get upset about that" or that it's not important in the over-all article. And he'd say "Well, it's me, not you. It does make a difference as to who that particular word may be written about, or that sentence may be talking about."

. . . he would take something out of a newspaper article

that he knew you had been working on and throw it up to you a day or two later . . . and he would say, "Weren't you handling this thing? Why didn't you give it more thought before this got in the papers?" or "Shouldn't this have been handled a litle differently?" There is something about the written word that I think is extremely sensitive to him.

I think Ted is thin-skinned when it comes to the written word as opposed to the verbal conversation sort of thing, because he can see it and dwells on it and it bothers him. But, I know I have seen things on TV that I would have gotten much more upset about than many of the things that he got concerned about, that were written, and I think there is something about the written word that far overshadows the verbal thing. You can say things to him that are no problem. But if you put it in writing you've got a problem.

There was, in Agnew's relationship with the press, a basic insecurity. Perhaps it was simply political insecurity. Dutch Moore recognized its practical aspects.

I think the press meant more to him than to the other politicians because he was from a minority party. This bothered him. He felt he had to be right as far as what was said in the press about him or his image. Being a member of a minority party, he couldn't afford not to have the press with [him]. I think every article he ever read, at least prior to becoming governor, he analyzed as to what is the average reader going to glean out of this article? How is my image going to come through with respect to this particular action or the manner in which the particular article was written? And I think the majority of it was being a Republican in a four-to-one Democratic area.

Added to this must be Agnew's own view of the press. He was not the product of a political machine or an effective political party. What he had gained, he believed, came from his careful manipulation of the press, which meant the press was responsible for everything he had in his life—his success up to that time, his community status, a reasonable income. Is it any wonder that he worried when he painfully learned that he could not control those who had given him everything and, by extension, could take everything away?

At the end of his first year as county executive, a *Sun* papers editorial recalled Agnew's initial appearance in such terms as a knight in shining armor, a new broom, and a breath of fresh air. Assessing this grab bag of metaphors, the editorial concluded, ". . . the broom has shed a few of its straws and the armor may be slightly tarnished but . . . [he] is still firmly mounted and busily tilting lances with all the problems of modern government." It was a rating high enough for a politician less demanding of praise than Agnew. If Agnew had run for re-election the *Sun* papers would have supported him, the county situation remained essentially the same, with the Democratic machine waiting to take over once more. However, in 1966 Agnew shifted his sights to the governor's seat and, except for the fortuitous circumstances of George Mahoney's Democratic primary win, the *Sun* papers probably would not have continued in its support of him.

Before Mahoney's nomination, Agnew faced major problems of promoting himself as a candidate in a heavily Democratic state politically segmented into areas of sharply divergent interests. He was unknown in all but the Baltimore area. He had to gain recognition, then support, and to draw on independents and Democrats if he hoped to win.

Mahoney's primary victory solved all these problems. The *Sun* papers supported him once again, and with fervor, in order to stop Mahoney.

Agnew's sweep from governor to potential vice-presidential candidate was so rapid that the images of him overlap. From the moment of his victory, he savored the taste of national publicity. The election of a Republican in a Democratic state was interesting enough to the trend-watchers to give him more than ordinary national attention. Furthermore, the votes that Mahoney had attracted in 1966 were considered to be the same as those that had gone to George Wallace in the Maryland presidential primary in 1964, which made the trend-watchers doubly interested. The jittery liberal obsession with the idea of a white backlash had made Agnew's campaign into a sign of possible salvation not only for the state, but possibly for the nation. Not only newspapers, but also the news magazines became interested in him. As governor, he was no longer the parochial politician he had been in Baltimore County. For, in Annapolis he now had the attention, not only of the *Sun* papers, the *News-American,* the three Baltimore television stations and several radio stations, but also of the Washington *Post,* the *Evening Star,* and the *News,* as well as all the Washington television and radio stations. In fact, on a good day there could be as many as twenty-five or thirty newsmen at the governor's command. As governor, he was a legitimate and sought after source of news. He no longer had to worry about the press coming to him. And the reporter asking to see him privately might just as likely be from the New York *Times* as from the Baltimore *Sun,* for it was hardly two months after his inauguration that he thrust himself into the national search for a Republican presidential candidate.

When Agnew was county executive, Edgar Jones got so many calls from him that he was known around his office as "Agnew's man." The new governor's inauguration was a turning point. Jones got no more calls after that. Governor Agnew, when he was on the phone, spoke only to the editor in chief. Sometimes the subject was the governor's dismay over a Jones editorial. "I don't know what his mental process was after he got to Annapolis," said Jones. Agnew probably had no better understanding of newspapers, but he did understand status. "Editor in chief" has a crystal ring that "editorial writer" lacks.

The spring of 1968 brought several events that were to change Agnew's attitude toward the press significantly. First came an excruciating debacle over the presidential candidacy of Nelson Rockefeller. In early March, Agnew arranged to have a color television set installed in his own conference room so that he could watch Rockefeller announce his candidacy. Agnew had been one of the first supporters of Rockefeller on this most recent presidential go-round and headed a national Rockefeller for President Committee. He invited the State House reporters in to watch him watching the announcement. There was a sense of history about the moment. Rockefeller might be president. Who knew for what important position Agnew, his early and strong supporter, might be tapped? Then, instead of the expected, there was a shocking surprise. To Agnew's dismay and embarrassment, Rockefeller announced he would not run. He had not bothered to inform Agnew of his decision, an omission that could scarcely be explained away to the reporters. The conclusion seemed to be obvious; Agnew really did not figure in Rocky's plans. It was a humiliating and depressing experience.

Two weeks later the Baltimore riot exploded. Agnew was now getting more national publicity than he could handle —and all bad. One might have thought that he would, therefore, have excluded the press from his post-riot meeting with the black leaders, in order to give his national image a rest. However, the track Agnew runs on is always one-way, and the way is forward. The meeting went on. Agnew's excellent television presence, his attention to colorful phrases and short, snappy thoughts that fit so well the television news time sequences, his sense of drama, importance and authority, all these elements were rolled up in one smashing virtuoso performance. There was nothing impromptu about his role. He had had ample time to reconsider as advisers, staff members, Mayor D'Alesandro—one after another had tried to get him to back off from another, inevitable personal disaster. But he said he was doing the right thing and he continued to insist he had done the right thing even after all those black leaders had stormed in anguish from the room.

And suddenly, despite the hostility of the press, there was an outpouring of telegrams, phone calls and letters from all over the state, and from other states as well. He knew he was right; now from everywhere there were thousands of others who said he was right, and kept saying it even after the editorials and news magazines and white clergymen and blacks all over America shouted out how wrong he was. Despite that condemnation from all the articulate sources that ought to have counted, here was this outpouring from people who were thinking for themselves and coming to the same conclusion that he did; and at the same time coming to the conclusion that he was one hell of a guy.

With that experience Agnew tore away the umbilical cord. For years he had adhered to some academic think-through that overemphasized the influence of the press and underestimated the independence of the public; that spoke of government being remote and of a citizenry that abrogated their decision-making responsibilities to the decision-makers, the hundreds of Edgar Joneses who held a remote control on public attitudes. But if this were true for a county executive it was no longer true for him. It was clear that he could do what he wanted, seek out his own supporters, and that he didn't need the support of the press to do it.

He had always relied on helping hands. The financial support of his father even after his marriage; the jobs that came through the friends of his father; the jobs and advice from a fatherly judge; the paternal protection of a powerful newspaper. The days following his lecture to the black leaders were like leaving home. It was marvelous and a fulfilling restoration for someone who had just suffered the rejection, the slap in the face, delivered by the governor of New York whose favor he had so fervently courted.

The press could sit back and make its judgments. He did not need its advice, only its news columns. And this was the final thing that Agnew learned about the press, something that was too elemental for him to believe in Baltimore County; a newspaper might hate him on its editorial pages and still give him space in the news columns. He hadn't understood this when Edgar Jones explained it, but he understands it now and understands that there is more than just some internal newspaper office policy involved. What is involved is the psychology of the press, that big permissive parent, full of self-doubt and guilt, and slightly masochistic, that parent that bends over backwards to be fair even to its most wayward children.

As Vice President, Agnew gets all of the space he should, which means that anytime he says something, the press will print it at a length determined by their professional judgment as to its importance and interest. To that is added all the extra space the liberal press tends to give to those it opposes, in order to avoid the charge that it discriminates anywhere but on the editorial page. Liberal reporters and news editors add to the coverage even more, because, cynics though they are, they labor in the belief that the more exposure is given to the ills of society, the more likely is the citizenry to turn to something better. Finally, there is the detailed coverage the press always gives to those who attack it directly; uneasily aware that its expensive, complicated, heavily equipped and undermanned business has become a private sanctuary for Freedom of the Press, it must be a platform for its own critics because there is no other platform.

For all of the above reasons, the press, caught in its own self-conscious power, compulsively gives more and more space to Agnew while they enjoy him less. It is the press's special weakness and it can do nothing about it. If Agnew is suppressed, he can claim that his charges are true. Only the obvious cranks of extreme psychotic disorientation get shut out, and not even these if they hold public office. The liberal press fears Agnew because it is instinctively alert to anything that hints of repressiveness. It does not fear the Vice President as a personal antagonist. No speech or action of his could harm the Washington *Post,* the New York *Times, Newsweek,* or the *Sun,* all of whom will be around as strong or stronger long after Agnew's political life has run its course.

Agnew knows all of these things about the press, and he goes after it as a jujitsu artist would, flipping, throwing, pinning, not through his own strength (a ninety-pound woman can throw a six-foot man, the jujitsu books claim), but by using the press's own stance, its own momentum and weight, to its own disadvantage. Thus when Agnew claimed that Averell Harriman sold out Poland to Stalin for two riding horses, the Washington *Post* found the charge so absurd it devoted nearly its entire editorial page to the matter.

Agnew has not figured out anything new. Governor Lester Maddox has been doing the same thing for years. But most effective politicians or government officials would feel demeaned by such tactics of publicity. Nor would they want to use up press and public attention, valuable assets that they are, on self-made issues, unprovoked attacks and aimless rattling around the body politic. On the other hand, real crooks cannot use Agnew's attention-getting devices. The press spots them and draws the line on them. The other run-of-the-mill sorts simply don't have the gall to do what Agnew does. They are not as shameless as he is. He has the playground largely to himself.

Agnew has now reached the high ground in his strategy for self-promotion; press criticism has become beneficial to him. The people he speaks to are happy to know that the New York *Times* and the Washington *Post* and the *Herald* in Rutland, Vermont, oppose what he says. What he says is enriched when it rankles the press and infuriates his detractors.

Agnew is to the national press what Lester Maddox is to the Atlanta *Constitution* and *Journal*—a burr they cannot get rid of, an irritation that attracts inordinate attention when there are so many more injurious and important things that need attention. Agnew no longer has to give the press any urban renewal issues to "eat up." He has the press just where he wants it.

"You know," said Scott Moore, "they criticized him when he ran for Vice President—became Vice President—about how green he was and so forth and so on. This is an absolute untruth. This guy had six years of experience before those television cameras before he was ever mentioned for Vice President, and there was nobody in the state of Maryland that was on television more than Agnew in that six-year period. And if anybody could ever learn—and he could learn and was pretty polished at television—it was Agnew . . . he had a lot of time on that subject."

15

AGNEW'S IMAGINED horizons have always stretched beyond the limitations of his immediate view; his first glimpse of politics on a national level appeared to him while he was occupied with the provincial duties of serving as Baltimore County Executive. In late 1963 and early 1964 he became engaged in a serious thrust to gain control of the county Republican party, still firmly in the hands of Fife Symington's faction. The struggle soon narrowed down to a fight for county delegates to the Republican state convention. The delegates were to be elected in a party primary in the county. At the state convention these local representatives would in turn elect the state's delegates to the national convention in San Francisco, instructing them and possibly committing them to one of the announced presidential candidates. Symington, deeply committed to conservatism, had finally found in Senator Barry Goldwater a candidate far enough to the right to be acceptable. Agnew did not favor Barry Goldwater, but of more immediate importance, he opposed Symington and Symington's strength in the party. Throughout that year the purely local fight for county party control was viewed by the press through the magnifying lens of national politics. And since Symington was a conservative with no doubts, a Goldwater man, Agnew, in his opposition to Symington-Goldwater, gained the labels of "progressive," "moderate" or "liberal," whichever seemed to its user to be the opposite of "conservative."

Eventually Agnew outmaneuvered the Symington forces and won a compromise which in fact constituted a total victory for him. The county Republicans united behind a single "official" slate of delegates which included eight named by Agnew and six named by Symington. The delegates, in addition, would go to the state convention uninstructed. With that compromise, the county party leadership passed from Symington to Agnew.

During that year Agnew got several further stimulating glimpses of national politics. In the spring of 1964, he joined a statewide delegation of Maryland Republicans who journeyed to Harrisburg to encourage Pennsylvania's Governor William W. Scranton to seek the Republican presidential nomination. The distance in miles from Towson to Harrisburg is not great, but the experience of petitioning a party member to run for the nation's highest office is exhilaratingly remote from sewage extensions and other routines of local government. Later Agnew would accept the chairmanship of the Maryland Scranton-for-President Committee, a not-so-exhilarating experience in that Scranton hovered uncertainly for several months, unable to make up his mind whether or not to descend to the level of presidential politics. In July Agnew attended the national convention itself. Then, disappointed with the nomination of Goldwater, he refrained from partisan politicking for the rest of the year, which, given the outcome of Goldwater's ill-fated campaign, did him no harm. 1964 was, in sum, a terrible year during which to be a Republican. To Agnew, however, it was a stimulating appetizer. As the next national election approached, he leaped in so early it seemed as though he were trying to be the first to herald the event. He clearly intended to become an active participant, capturing as large a role for himself as he could.

Agnew was sworn in as governor of Maryland in January 1967. By May he had publicly announced his preference for Governor Nelson Rockefeller as the next Republican presidential nominee, having already scouted out the prospects of governors Romney of Michigan and James Rhodes of Ohio. It hardly makes much sense, this sudden boyish springtime plunge into the onrushing political river. But perhaps Agnew saw himself as closer to greatness than one would usually expect of a newly elected governor of a small state. Assuming that the next nominee was to come from the ranks of Republican governors in the nation, Agnew was clearly not an obvious potential candidate himself, but there was no reason why among the other twenty-one he could not work his way to the top—chief among the supporters of the candidates, if not a candidate himself.

Agnew eagerly attended the Republican governors' conference and just as eagerly accepted the routine invitations extended by the other governors for Agnew to speak in their states. Throughout the rest of the year and on into 1968, Agnew repeatedly described Rockefeller as "the best-qualified candidate possible for the presidency." By early 1968, a visitor from out-of-state would have thought that the news coverage of the Republican national party was being given a rather odd slant in Maryland. Looking at Maryland newspapers and viewing local television stations, the impression received was that the man closest to what was happening nationally was Spiro T. Agnew.

Agnew, it seemed, was on his way to becoming the king-maker in the coming election. His press conferences were filled with questions about the Rockefeller candidacy, with sometimes as many as half the questions devoted to that topic.

By March, ten months after Agnew had started boosting him, Rockefeller was still assessing his own chances as a candidate and had not announced his intentions. But if Agnew's early and eager endorsement of him had seemed opportunistic and politically naïve, at this point it suddenly began to pay off. With the encouragement of people close to the New York governor, Agnew announced the formation of a "National Rockefeller '68 Committee" which would have its headquarters in Annapolis and Agnew himself as temporary chairman. That announcement was made March 17; the committee held its first meeting the following day in Washington to discuss plans for coordinating the national movement. There was no question in any Marylander's mind that Agnew was leading the leader; by now even the national press treatment of Agnew's position conformed to the local coverage. It was a position of prominence destined to last for exactly three days.

On March 21 Governor Rockefeller was scheduled to hold a nationally televised press conference, and there was a heady excitement in Annapolis. Agnew's own regular weekly press conference coincided with the Rockefeller press conference in Albany. He had had no word from Governor Rockefeller, but he was certain that the coming announcement would be a formal statement of candidacy. His staff and the State House reporters would be able to watch Rockefeller's appearance on the television set Agnew had had installed in his conference room; then he would answer questions about the national campaign for Rockefeller that he was heading. The Maryland press would have the novel opportunity of waching the national campaign chairman's reaction as his candidate tossed his hat into the ring.

The experience was more novel than anyone expected. As Rockefeller announced that he would not, in fact, be a candidate, the Maryland political reporters (as well as the television camera brought for the event) recorded Agnew's distress. He was not merely caught by surprise, embarrassed and offended, but, through his own eagerness, had seen to it that he was on public display as the governor of New York went his own way without so much as a courtesy nod to the governor of Maryland.

When the Rockefeller telecast ended, Agnew turned to the reporters gathered with him. His usual articulateness failed him: "First of all, I think what the Governor said today is that he meant it several months ago, and as he said consistently, that he will not be a candidate for the nomination. . . . I confess that I am tremendously surprised. I also frankly add that I am greatly disappointed, because as an advocate and enthusiast for his candidacy, a person who has seen the sentiment that's being expressed over the country, and I felt that there was a good chance that he could enter the campaign actively without becoming divisive to the party. Apparently he doesn't feel this way." When a reporter inquired if Agnew would support Nixon as the nominee, the governor replied, "I have indicated that Mr. Nixon is a very acceptable candidate to me and in fact said on several occasions he may be my second choice." In all there were only five quick questions in that press conference and the reporters left to tell the state and the nation the ghastly details of the incident.

By morning, Agnew was a laughing stock in political circles. He had been acting as kingmaker, yet all along he had been beneath the notice of the king-to-be. He had leaped on what he thought would be a bandwagon, jettisoning whatever political weight he might have carried by playing the possible candidates against one another. He had thought that being first would bring him the best shot at national recognition and political rewards. It was a headstrong gamble. He had lost. And he had compounded his lack of judgment by enabling the press to witness the exact moment of humiliation. However glum he felt, and despite the moodiness that was apparent to his staff, he did not show it publicly.

The shame and bewilderment of the press conference was a momentary lapse. When he recovered, he came back with as much nervy self-confidence as ever. Less than a week later, Nixon, seeing an opportunity to take advantage of Rockefeller's snub of Agnew, sent the Maryland governor an invitation to meet him in New York to discuss the party and the coming primary. "I want to get a greater understanding of his [Nixon's] position on domestic affairs," Agnew told the press, as if the Rockefeller incident had never happened. Agnew's attitude made clear that the Nixon invitation was a bid for his support (which in truth it was) and that he was still in there, importantly deciding where to throw his weight for the sake of the party, the nation, even history. "I am not really clear in my own mind where he stands on the problems of urban areas and other vital domestic considerations," Agnew said, with a weighty seriousness that bordered on pomp. Later, as vice-presidential candidate and as Vice President, Agnew would demonstrate this same imperviousness to public ridicule and criticism, an almost inhuman placidity and confidence in the backwash of his own errors, whether gross or picayune.

The fact is that Agnew was being taken seriously, almost as seriously as he was viewing himself. The Republican governors intended to play a major role in the selection of the presidential nominee. The twenty-four states in Republican hands collectively represented a majority of the electoral votes. And even though the party's national committee was controlled by the GOP powers in Congress, the governors controlled the party in the states and precincts where the votes were counted. In their book, *The Republican Establishment,* published in 1967, Stephen Hess and David Broder listed five Republican governors described as the "answer to victory for the GOP in 1968," and Agnew was among them. When Agnew

158)) *Robert Marsh*

did meet with Nixon on March 30, 1968, the New York *Times,* referring to him as a liberal, noted Agnew's potential importance to the Nixon campaign. And so, in remarkably quick time, Agnew was back on the track, with his ego restoked, even if the track was a different one, running in a new direction. From that first meeting with Nixon, Agnew began throwing the switches that would move him, by August, from Rockefeller's camp to Nixon's. And before midsummer, Agnew was evaluating his chances, not merely as a key Nixon supporter, but as a running mate if Nixon won the nomination.

No honest act of a politician is so secret as the process of selecting a vice-presidential candidate. Ultimately it is the sole decision of the presidential candidate, a determination resting on his own assessment of which man can do him the most good. But the process is one of elimination as well as selection, and a public discussion of the factors putting many men aside can be more harmful politically than the rationale for the choice itself.

The dos-à-dos that Nixon danced with every segment of the Republican party before choosing his running mate is well known. In fact, Nixon's staff made certain it would be well known by releasing a running account of what purported to be the selection process even as it was taking place. Fifty prominent Republicans met privately with Nixon in small, carefully balanced groups to submit names to him and to discuss the men being considered for the ticket. There were more than a dozen such names, from the "glamor candidates," such as Mayor John Lindsay of New York and Governor Ronald Reagan of California, through prominent senators and obscure congressmen. Throughout a series of meetings the night of August 8 and into the early morning hours of August 9, the list narrowed as Nixon, seemingly acting as impartial arbiter, conducted his search for a consensus candidate, agreeable to Northern liberals and the kind of Southerners typified by South Carolina Senator Strom Thurmond. With each group, objections of various sorts eliminated all but two or three names, one of which was Spiro T. Agnew, governor of Maryland, seemingly the most inconsequential of the lot. Eventually, as if by true consensus, the man arrived at was Governor

Agnew, a man who, in fact, no one wanted in the number two spot except Richard M. Nixon himself.

Nixon had extended to Agnew in early June the possibility that he might have a spot on the ticket. John Mitchell, now Attorney General, and the mastermind of the Nixon campaign, had given Agnew's background a quick check well before the delegates convened in Miami Beach. Agnew had, it turned out, been given a running start for the job as early as that first meeting with Nixon the week after Rockefeller's televised withdrawal. That meeting was arranged by Maryland State Senator Louise Gore, a wealthy Montgomery County conservative and a close friend of Strom Thurmond, a connection that was, as it turned out, just exactly right for the 1968 Republican convention. Throughout the summer there were more meetings between Nixon and Agnew. Despite all of the unkind, uncomplimentary quips and jokes by Nixon staff members which leaked to the press, Agnew had impressed the boss himself from the start. Nixon had an early, strong, favorable impression of Agnew's mind, his thinking processes and his ideas, that few other people shared. One observer, commenting on this first impression, said of Agnew, "He fooled me for a few weeks. He seems to take in data very quickly and has a couple of ideas that seem to suggest he might have an original mind. . . . Nixon probably extracted those few ideas of Agnew's and thought there might be more in the pipeline. He couldn't have been more mistaken."

Nixon probably extended the possibility of the vice-presidency to many men as the tug of war between the vice-presidential candidates continued into midsummer. But Agnew took his own chances seriously. Although he made no more public announcements about his intentions, he began edging closer to Nixon. So close that when the Rockefeller drive began to get steam up again after President Johnson's withdrawal from the election, Agnew could muster no interest in the effort. Rockefeller, he had said, was the best man the Republicans could offer, but the affront Agnew suffered at Rocky's hands, contrasted with the blandishments of Nixon, quickly made such objective appraisals subsidiary to other concerns. Agnew was no longer Rockefeller's man. That was clear. But whose man was he? He didn't say, but Maryland's blacks claimed they got an early message. Being blacks, they were more sensitive to the metamorphosis that was taking place, to Agnew's springtime emergence as a radical conservative.

The precipitating incident was the Baltimore riot; the actual emergence from the chrysalis came with his confrontation of the black leaders. That meeting represented no about-face or sudden change in Agnew's views, but rather the public emergence of his fundamental feelings from the cocoon of platitudinous "morality." In their analysis of the 1968 presidential campaign, *An American Melodrama* (by Lewis Chester, Godfrey Hodgson and Bruce Page), the authors comment in this fashion about Agnew's selection at the convention:

> But the little that was known about him pleased the South. For Agnew's chief political distinction in the course of the year had been to start out as a racial liberal and arrive at midsummer, in the wake of the spring riots, as Mr. Backlash in person.

That, of course, is a white man's view of Agnew. To the Maryland black man, with a stronger memory for such things, whatever Agnew is—Mr. Backlash, Mr. Law and Order, whoever—he has always been. There was, for example, the intriguing, prescient remark of Walter Lively, the Baltimore black militant, who, in July 1967, claimed that Agnew's hard line and massive use of force in the Cambridge disturbances arose because of Agnew's vice-presidential ambitions. For any political purposes that he might wish to serve, Agnew had a consistent law and order position to recall. What the black leaders' meeting gave him was a chance to make that position known nationally.

Clarence Mitchell, a Maryland black state senator, sums up this view of the political motivation of Agnew's dressing down of the black leaders: "I got the impression that it was a setup—as I look back now—that Agnew had decided—knew—he couldn't be re-elected governor because he was too liberal for the conservatives in the state and had not been liberal enough, and a disappointment to the liberals and to the black community in the state. So that he knew he had to go someplace else. And I made [sic] the opinion at that time that he was trying to jockey for a Cabinet position . . . if Nixon had the possibility of success. The fact that he had initiated Republicans for Rockefeller and had gone to all of the lengths that he had gone to, to try to get that movement off the ground, and then, when Rockefeller withdrew, of course this took his hopes away. I felt then he was trying to get a position with the Rockefeller administration in anticipation that Rockefeller would actually run. After he couldn't do that, he was looking around again, and figures, 'Well, I'm only left with Nixon.' And he knew . . . the one thing Nixon needed was a person who had a conservative enough image to campaign throughout the South to help him deliver the South. So that Agnew brought in all the national news media."

All the people around Agnew, his staff people, his friends, and his political associates argue that Agnew never—or rarely—considered the political consequences of his actions or statements at such times, even in the face of such large issues as the Baltimore riot, and all argue that there were no political considerations in Agnew's mind when he spoke to the black leaders. Certainly what Agnew said to them was predictable. What is intriguing, as Senator Mitchell notes, is his having addressed them publicly. Would he have done so if Rockefeller, two weeks before, had announced that he was a candidate rather than that he was not? Would Rockefeller have had to use the vice-presidential spot to balance his ticket and offset his own liberalism with a law-and-order candidate? If Nixon were to be the candidate, many argued that he would need a man who could appease the Northern liberals and the blacks. Did Agnew figure as early as April that Nixon would, in fact, look southward, because he could in no way win blacks or liberals? The problem was a complex one, and many more experienced political observers misjudged the outcome. If, however, Agnew's decision to call in the press and the television crewmen to witness his chastisement of the blacks was without political considerations (and the evidence and logic of the situation seems weighted toward that conclusion), then the decision was one of the most remarkable examples of how Agnew's rash acts, taken against the best advice of those around him, ultimately worked in his favor. The letters and telegrams that poured in congratulating him on that bit of speechmaking conclusively demonstrated that he was acceptable to the only group Nixon had to worry about not offending. In the final analysis, Nixon would not balance his ticket but would fill the number two position with a person as close as possible to his own image. Nixon himself, the polls showed, could be elected President, therefore he needed no help in getting votes. What he needed was someone who would not lose him votes; next to leaving the Number Two position vacant, the best alternative was Agnew.

This reasoning seemed too coldly calculating for those analysts who think traditionally in terms of a national constituency, a broad platform appealing to every region, economic group and social class. And so, as the convention got under way, the press, liberal and traditional, looked everywhere but to Agnew for a vice-presidential choice. (The single important exception was David Broder of the Washington *Post.*) By this time, nevertheless, the choice had been made, and barring unforeseen circumstances, the announcement of Agnew would inevitably follow.

The Maryland delegation went to Miami pledged to Agnew as a favorite son. Agnew already had won, as a tangible sign of Nixon's interest in him, the role of delivering Nixon's nominating speech. That supporting role is not usually a good stepping stone to a vice-presidential nomination; in fact, it is just the reverse—it gives a man, a governor or senator who has helped a great deal and deserves some payoff, a token recognition of his services because he is not going to get anything else. But Agnew, in his entire career, was always standing on unlikely platforms when he launched himself into new offices. The nominating speech does provide, for a dazzling half hour or so, the ultimate focus of national attention. And if the speaker is good, the publicity is enormous. Agnew wanted this spotlight, felt he needed the national attention as well as the prominent appearance before the delegates. Perhaps he counted on being impressive. He wasn't impressive, but he did get the attention he needed (and which Nixon wanted him to have) and he did not hurt himself in any way by what he said or by his delivery. In a dull, ponderous convention he fit in neatly.

The nominating speech was actually Agnew's second prominent appearance at the convention. Prior to this, Agnew had announced his abdication as favorite son and his support of Nixon. The announcement was carefully timed and strategically placed. It came as Nixon himself was arriving in Miami. The candidate and his wife remained aboard their plane for ten minutes after it landed so that their entrance to the city, awaited by press and television cameras, would immediately follow, but not cut into, Agnew's statement of support. It was a prelude to the convention itself; Agnew introducing Nixon's arrival to the convention city as he would Nixon's entrance into the actual balloting. No one was paying such attention to the signs at the time, but Agnew had been programmed into the Nixon scenario from curtain rise to final bows.

Agnew denies he had advance warning of his selection. So do all of his own staff. Nixon himself, of course, insisted at the convention that "I brought no names to Miami." One Nixon staff member, however, confirms that the choice was Nixon's alone and was Nixon's no later than mid-July, when Agnew also knew that he was the probable choice. Ten days before going to Miami, Agnew had confided to one person, his golfing partner Judge Lester Barrett of Baltimore, about his "possible chances" of getting the nomination. Agnew, in his acceptance speech, told the delegates, "I honestly had no idea that I would be back on this platform to accept this nomination tonight."

"I stand here with a deep sense of the improbability of this moment," he said. It was a feeling shared by the entire nation, and particularly by those people who knew him best in Maryland, even though they really should not have found anything improbable in a career so dogged by luck.

16

PERHAPS THE MOST audacious remark ever uttered by Vice President Spiro T. Agnew was a reference he made in spring 1970 to "my ancestor Aristotle." It is hard to imagine another figure in human history as unrelated to Agnew as that ancient Greek systematic thinker. Agnew is neither philosopher nor systematic thinker. He has not shown himself to have deep commitments of any sort, personal, political, or sociological. He is very much like his boss, President Nixon, neither liberal nor conservative, and so politically elusive that he is often simultaneously a disappointment to his supporters and an exasperation to his detractors.

Agnew is not a pragmatic politician who works for what he assesses as realistic and obtainable successes. Nor is he the kind of skilled professional careerist whose actions and public positions are determined solely by the prevailing winds. His personality intrudes so much on his public decision-making that in some cases those decisions have the appearance of attempted political suicide. "Political eunuch" was the label pinned on him by Nixon staff members when he was being considered for the ticket. And in truth, it is vain to look back through Agnew's record for evidence of political convictions.

Perhaps the only issue to which he really committed himself was that of the urban renewal program in Baltimore County. And urban renewal was an issue whose implications he did not understand. To him it was simply a plan for industrial development, and he was both shocked and puzzled when voters started raising such broad issues as the constitutional rights of property and free enterprise, to say nothing of shouting slogans about socialism and communism. Agnew had no idea that an urban renewal program could raise constitutional questions.

Edgar Jones, who wrote on local government for the

editorial page of the *Sun*, recalls the following incident.

> On so many issues he [Agnew] was just kind of naïve, I felt. Urban renewal is one that comes to my mind. . . . I didn't realize how little he knew about it until a luncheon when he was really in a high degree of distress because of the opposition to this thing and what the opposition was saying. And he brought out this flyer and said, "Look what they're saying! I've got to find some way to stop this! What they're saying is that this is a plan to take property away from the people who now have it and turn it over to somebody else to use for their private profit!" Well, that's exactly what urban renewal does. This was completely shocking to him. This was contrary to what he considered to be the facts. He hadn't been in urban renewal long enough, or he hadn't gone back to see the origins of urban renewal—the purpose, the philosophy, and why it was that it would be considered in the public interest to assemble parcels of land which, true enough, had belonged to somebody else and make parcels large enough that you could sell to somebody who wanted to put up office buildings and shopping centers and all that. So that what he thought was just a damnable lie about the urban renewal program [was true]. And actually, to take it from these people and sell it to somebody else at a reduced price, you know! There's a whole set of governmental principles involved in why you do this and there's a whole set of court tests in the background. But he came in at the top and all he saw in the urban renewal plan, essentially, was its being something that was going to increase the county tax base by fourteen million dollars, and therefore help the property tax, and all that. But he just didn't know enough about urban renewal to know how to defend it well.

Those who have come to know Agnew in his role as Vice President, view him as a political conservative, mistaking mere reflections of his personality for extreme political views. Personally, the national Agnew is the same man he always was, but magnified now by the larger role he plays in a wider arena. His positions, however, are those of the Nixon administration. When he differs, or seems to differ, from the administration, he is often further to the right. But in nearly every case this right-wing tone develops out of the statement of an administration position in bolder words. Agnew has come to be the administration cheerleader and Number One Fan. As Agnew knows, being a committed sports fan himself, when a fan yells "kill him" to the athlete in the ring, he does not mean it literally. He only means to encourage the athlete (Nixon) to continue doing what he is doing as hard as he can. To those unfamiliar with Agnew's past, it is difficult to envision him as anything but an ultra-conservative; he seems to fit the role and he seems to enjoy it so much. But Agnew's past is clear proof that he would be shouting "kill him" just as loudly if Nixon suddenly decided to nationalize General Motors.

Agnew's very first significant political act—joining the Republican party—did not stem from conviction but from personal ambition. He didn't think he had a chance in politics as a Democrat. The competition was too great. He lacked the background, the education, the connections. The Democratic party is the big leagues in Maryland. Judge Barrett, whom Agnew credits with influencing him to switch parties, gives this assessment of the change. "Of course it was important that he did change his politics, because in Baltimore County there were so many outstanding Democrats who sought office and comparatively few Republicans. So that his opportunity to be a major candidate was much better in the Republican party than in the Democratic party." But it was also true, of course, that Agnew's chances of *winning* an office as a Republican were far slimmer. In any event, he did not become a Republican because of any values the party stood for locally or nationally.

Later, Agnew's personal opposition to Fife Symington, the conservative in Baltimore County politics, prompted the newspapers to tag him, carelessly, with the "liberal" label. Some other choices that Agnew made did place him, more legitimately, on that side of the political spectrum. One of the most surprising, in retrospect, is his endorsement of Thomas L. Kuchel as a likely presidential candidate in 1964. Agnew was county executive then and Kuchel was senior senator from California and the Senate minority whip. Kuchel's voting record placed him slightly left of the Republican center, but well within the midstream of American politics. Nevertheless, he had a reputation as a liberal; called "a Republican extremist" by Barry Goldwater, he was one of the earliest California backers of the 1964 candidacy of Governor Nelson Rockefeller. For a brief time, Kuchel's name was mentioned as a Republican possibility in a list that included a half dozen more likely candidates, Govenor Rockefeller, Senator Goldwater, Governor George Romney of Michigan, Governor William Scranton of Pennsylvania, and Henry Cabot Lodge. Later, Agnew switched his inclinations to Governor Scranton. Finally, his feuding with Fife Symington over control of the county party resulted in a holding action that prevented Symington from swinging the county party delegates over to the support of Senator Goldwater. That delegate fight was ideological on Symington's part, personal on Agnew's, but even so Senator Goldwater apparently held no attractions for Agnew. In 1968, as we have seen, Agnew was an early Rockefeller backer.

Taken together, the early choices Agnew made in both of these national elections could be construed as an indication of his basic tendency toward liberalism; it is more likely, however, that he was leaning toward the potential winner. Goldwater's capture of the nomination was unforeseen in early 1964, as was Nixon's political comeback in 1968; Agnew's early money on liberal candidates reflected the best odds in the minds of most political experts. It must be emphasized that Agnew showed no interest in party politics as such; if the personal role he had chosen for himself did not work out, his commitment flagged. He served as chairman of the Scranton campaign in Maryland, but after Goldwater's victory, having no personal credit with the Goldwater forces and therefore no role of importance open to him, his interest in national politics lapsed until 1968. If he seems to be a team man and a party man now that he is Vice President, it is a new role for him. As county executive he did nothing to build the county Republican party, and as governor he accomplished little for the state party.

Agnew is, as one associate called him, the Great Single

Shooter, meaning that when at the top of the ticket he looks out only for himself. This kept him from any meaningful attachments to his party and any commitments to issues per se. In addition, Agnew has a personal approach to decision-making which is nearly vacuum-sealed. He has said, "A dozen opposing views can't change my mind when I have a strong feeling about them." These three elements, then, determine his positions: the lack of a broad thoughtful (philosophic) base to his politics, his Single Shooter attitude toward advancing his own career, and his personal sense of the "rightness" of his instincts. How could he be anything but unpredictable, given these determining factors?

Agnew's early political friends generously apply the label of "moderate" to Agnew, meaning that he is neither to the right nor to the left of center. Senator Glenn Beall, who was a leader of the Maryland Republican Party on the state level when it endorsed Agnew for governor, speaks of him in this fashion: ". . . it depends on the context at the time. It's all relative to that. He was a reform candidate in Baltimore County because reform was what was needed at the time, probably. He was a liberal because he was running against George Mahoney. He was a conservative compared with Hubert Humphrey and Ed Muskie. I think, therefore, he is a moderate. A true middle-of-the-road person."

Any man who is so completely defined by his surroundings, however, cannot properly be said to have earned any label at all.

Marshall Jones, a black politician in Baltimore, describes Agnew like this: "He was a Rockefeller man. And then he became a lukewarm Rockefeller man. Then he became a Nixon man. And then he became a strong Nixon man. He went with the breeze; he went with the wind. Political winds dictated to him." Interestingly enough, however, no one accuses him of being insincere. And he is sincere, having that remarkable, but not uncommon, political faculty of firmly believing everything that he says. ("Then you should say what you mean," the March Hare went on. "I do," Alice hastily replied; "at least—at least I mean what I say—that's the same thing, you know." "Not the same thing a bit!" said the Hatter.)

As Vice President, Agnew's success, if it can be called that, has come from the injection of himself into the issue of public dissent, whether it be dissent over civil rights, the conflict in Southeast Asia, or students' rights. Even his attacks on the press have centered around his views of proper dissent. On this matter Agnew has been consistent and if he can now be said to hold any firm beliefs about government, they might fall into that imprecise but understandable category "law and order." Agnew has added nothing to the dialogue concerning dissent aside from statements of his personal views, which he justifies more in terms of emotions than of reason. The issue, to him, is simple: there is no justification for demonstrations and civil disobedience. He does not understand the complexities that provoke dissenters into peaceful and not-so-peaceful public acts of protest. Civil disobedience leads to other forms of criminality, he has said. Civil rights demonstrations lead to civil disorder and to riots, he notes, making no distinction in his mind between lawbreaking for profit and lawbreaking for principle.

Local government trudges along in fixed ways that rarely raise broad political questions. An exception, however, is provided by the civil rights struggle, which has touched government at all levels. Agnew does have a record on this issue, as defined by his handling of the many civil rights confrontations that faced his county and state administrations. Although Agnew always insists that laws must be obeyed without exception in order to maintain order, he has often displayed an annoyance, even an anger, in the course of civil rights confrontations that indicates it is the affront to his personal authority rather than the violation of a governmental precept that he finds so distressing. In any event, Agnew does not recognize the special problems of minorities as justification for circumventing the normal processes of government, no matter how slow, ineffective or unresponsive those processes may be. This, of course, makes him no friend of the blacks. The Reverend Marion Bascomb of Baltimore, a civil rights activist who has come in contact with Agnew on many issues, charges Agnew with a lack of understanding and a lack of sympathy:

I think he has a certain basic cultural limitation. By this I mean that I am not sure that he understands the sociology, psychology, indeed the legality, of what black people are seeking. I think, and I say this very tenderly because every man is the child of his own culture, I just don't think Mr. Agnew had the advantage of a sophisticated background which enables him to understand certain problems. . . . You would have to know him as a black man, because in politics, here is a science of accommodating, [and] with black people at certain points there is no accommodating, there is no point in saying, "we will sell you this piece today at such and such a price, we can wait this out" . . . with black people there is an impatience which I don't think Mr. Agnew could understand. . . . In fact, as far as I'm concerned, anything . . . that he might have done is eclipsed by his ineptness and his total inability to understand the black problems and to enter into conversation, dialogue. He was always in the arena of debate. But, you see, I make the fine distinction that there is a difference between dialogue and debate; with debate you can argue some points, with dialogue you try to find out what is on the mind of the other person, rather than try to give him a shot in the arm with your own medicine.

I think he has a political philosophy. I think he thinks he is 150 per cent American.

To the black leaders of Maryland, the lack of understanding they saw in Agnew was not academic. It contributed, they say, to the slow pace of racial progress and to the increase in racial strife. ("He [Agnew] did more to polarize the black and white community in this state than anybody in the past," said Senator Mitchell.)

To Agnew, the fair housing law was a major accomplishment. Mr. Bascomb thinks there was a chance that Agnew could have prevented the eruption of violence in Cambridge. "We went down to see him once, when Rap Brown was at Cambridge. I think we initiated it [the meeting]. He never initiated anything after he became governor, this has to be remembered. We told him that as governor, he, in all probability, could have called the authorities, he could have spoken to Rap Brown because it had not gone that far." Mr. Bascomb claims that Agnew's obtuseness affected the influence of the black leaders themselves. "If Mr. Agnew had used different tactics with the black spokesmen in the community, in all probability our voices might not have been muted during the [Baltimore] rebellion. But because many people had taken our word that Mr. Agnew was this or that or the other, he had proved that he was not this to them, in their opinion. And therefore [when] we went out to try to stop looting and so forth, we had a credibility gap of our own."

The civil rights issue has run through Agnew's career mainly by his own choice. He made it a part of his campaign for county executive in order to attract the approval of the *Sun* papers. It was on the issue of civil rights that Agnew became an alternative to George Mahoney and won the governorship. And if there were no positive reasons for Agnew's selection as Nixon's running mate, the Vice President soon cut out a spot for himself by articulating the administration's sympathies with the white South and the white blue collar class, those groups most beleaguered by Negro demands for jobs, housing and better schooling.

"I think that Agnew thinks of Patrick Henry as a hero when he says, 'Give me liberty or give me death,'" said the Reverend Mr. Bascomb. "But he cannot understand Rap Brown's actions as being the same thing: 'Give me liberty or give me death.'" Mr. Bascomb is right; on this issue—rebellion, whether by fire bombs or sit-ins—Agnew's position is clear and consistent. We do not know how he feels about foreign trade, about fiscal policies or other international or national matters about which a potential President might some day be concerned. But we do know that never in his lifetime will any black activist, whether a street fighter or a congressman, be equated with Patrick Henry. On this he can be pinned down rather precisely.

Thus, the only area in which Agnew can be said to have a consistent, philosophic position, is civil dissent. And his position on that issue is a profoundly negative one.

17

SPIRO T. AGNEW appears to have invented a new mode of politics—upward mobility through failure; indeed he has proved the Peter Principle in reverse. Although he wanted to remain on the county board of appeals, he had antagonized the county council to the point where they refused to reappoint him. So he ran for county executive and won by default against a machine boss.

Although the county had wanted a reform candidate and might have preferred keeping the Democratic machine out of office, Agnew antagonized so many voters by his misjudging of issues that he had no hope of re-election. So he ran for governor and won by default against the blatantly racist campaign of a perennial loser.

As governor, however, he did nothing to cement the support of the blacks and white liberals who had elected him, but rather, in two short years antagonized those voters beyond recall. But halfway through the term he was called away to join the Nixon ticket, which won a narrow victory.

Many of his old political associates believe that Agnew is a terrible politician, but none can bring themselves to say it. After all, in politics winning carries its own proof:

Dutch Moore: "There was a time I thought that Ted was probably the worst politician in Baltimore County. As far as handling people and doing the right thing politically. Obviously, he is Vice President today, so my analysis of what kind of politician the guy is is obviously wrong."

Edgar Jones: "As a man who didn't think he was ready to become governor and certainly didn't think he was ready to become Vice President, I don't think I can say what his political future is. He is obviously a lucky man."

Dutch Moore: "Anybody could have beaten Mike Birmingham, who was all but on his deathbed in Baltimore County with the faction that was waiting in the wings to take over . . . anybody could have beaten George Mahoney. . . . I think that one thing that many people overlook is . . . not only the fact that he was in the right place at the right time, but he did have something to offer the people and this made it much more easy."

As a politician, Agnew has almost seemed like those distracted heroes of slapstick comedies who made all the wrong moves, stooping to pick up their hats when the villain is charging at them, but escaping the assault through their own ineptitude as the heavy, carried by his own momentum, goes sailing out the window.

All of Agnew's old associates are fascinated by the setbacks Agnew suffered which ultimately propelled him along in his career.

Sam Kimmel: "Now you know the history of how Ted could have been kept on the board of zoning appeals and would not have been Vice President. . . . If a deal had been worked out for the zoning board, I think he would have stayed on the zoning board." Or, it could equally well be said, if his law practice had thrived instead of foundered. Or if urban renewal had been adopted instead of defeated and he had remained county executive.

Judge Barrett has a private story of his own to tell. When, as county executive, Agnew began to realize he could not get re-elected, his thoughts did not turn immediately toward the gubernatorial race. Instead, he began brooding once more about being a judge, even though it already seemed possible that he could get his party's endorsement in the race for governor. Agnew spoke about his plans to Judge Barrett, saying that he still preferred a judgeship to running for governor. This was before George Mahoney's defeat of the regular party candidates in the Democratic primary, and Agnew's chances of success were unforeseeable, indeed, not all that bright. It seemed clear that Attorney General Finan, a close friend of the incumbent governor, Millard Tawes, would get the regular Democratic party endorsement and most likely the nomination. If Agnew did enter the race, Finan would be his opponent. Judge Barrett met with a member of Finan's staff and said that Agnew was planning to run for governor, but that he was interested in be-coming a judge and if he received a judgeship he probably would not run for governor. The implication was clear. By offering Agnew a place on the bench, Governor Tawes could eliminate Finan's strongest potential Republican opponent. The aide carried the information to Finan and Finan's response was, "Who's Agnew?" Agnew was no barrier to the governor's seat; a Republican rarely was. The message worked its way back through Judge Barrett to Agnew and, having no place else to go, Agnew entered the gubernatorial race. Finan, who lost to Mahoney in the primary, was appointed a judge by Governor Tawes after the primary and often when Judge Barrett meets Judge Finan, he reminds him of the time he asked, "Who's Agnew?"

It was not superior accomplishment in local and state office, or skilled political craftsmanship that made Agnew Vice President. In his first year as county executive and again as governor, both press and public generally regarded Agnew as a competent administrator; but then he seemed to wind down. Perhaps he lost interest; perhaps, having fulfilled the ambition of achieving the given office, his inner drives waned.

During his first year as county executive, Agnew was able to accomplish most of what he had promised in his campaign. He received credit for inaugurating a long-range formula for fi-nancing sewer and water extensions, a better system of records management, an open spaces law and conflict-of-interest regula-tions. Agnew sponsored or endorsed the creation of some new governmental agencies, such as a human relations commission, and some study groups, such as a zoning revision committee. Generally, however, these improvements were unremarkable for an executive who came into office as a reformer. It is true that he had to work with a county council controlled by mem-bers of the opposition party, but on the other hand, his election had been a clear enough message that the voters were repudiat-ing boss politics and were insisting on some change. Agnew, however, was not an inspired leader, and he was neither experi-enced enough nor diplomatic enough to win much council support.

Immediately after his election, Agnew exhibited a great deal of energy and perseverance studying the government he had been elected to head; he made a real effort to fulfill his campaign promises and he was praised for the quality of his appointments. But at the end of his one-year honeymoon, he slipped into a stage of indifference. The county council tightened its resistance to him, and he got less from them. He turned more responsibility and work over to his subordinates and spent more of his time on public disputes, which often were of no consequence. The only dispute of real importance was over the urban renewal program; here Agnew committed himself so deeply at the start that he was unable to back down without loss of face once the strength of the opposition became apparent. He went down with the program; but although this issue ruined his chances of re-election in the county, it was a plus in a statewide race, especially against George Mahoney. And so be became governor.

As governor, Agnew's record was quite similar to that during his term as county executive—mediocre to average in accomplishments, disastrous politically. He settled in Annapolis, having had no experience with state government, with no knowledge of the bureaucratic jungle, no acquaintanceship with most state employees or elected officials, and with the handicap of his membership in the minority Republican party.

Agnew was sworn in as governor in January 1967 as the legislative session for that year got underway. He resigned, after his election as Vice President, on January 7, 1969, two years later. Agnew himself summed up those two years in his farewell address to the Maryland General Assembly. It was a fairly candid assessment; upon further analysis, the record is even bleaker.

Agnew noted that in his inaugural address he had spoken of three broad goals for Maryland—fiscal reform, administrative reorganization and modernization of the state constitution. He continued, "The first we have achieved, the second is well underway and the third has failed." Actually, his plan for administrative reorganization was largely scrapped, leaving one goal achieved out of three. And even that victory was a dubious one. The state had been toying with the idea of fiscal reform for several years. Eventually a commission was formed to wrestle with the problem and a reform plan—the Cooper-Hughes plan (named after two of its authors)—was proposed. Agnew, as

Baltimore County Executive, had appeared at the hearings on the plan, and had made a strong pitch for suburbia. The problems of the small rural communities and the rural counties differed from those of the suburban counties; Baltimore city represented a third set of problems. Agnew argued forcefully for his suburban county, pointing to its rapid expansion and the imposing burdens on governmental services and facilities. What held true for Baltimore County held true also for Prince Georges and Montgomery, surrounding the District of Columbia. In the resulting compromises between the differing interests of Baltimore City, the suburban counties and the rural counties, the real reform purpose of the bill was largely sifted out. The Cooper-Hughes plan was defeated by the legislature. The following year, with Agnew as governor, the plan resurfaced as the Agnew-Hughes bill and this time it was passed. But, although Agnew termed it "fiscal reform" in his farewell address, it was, in fact, something far more pedestrian. Baltimore's Mayor D'Alesandro says, "The Agnew-Hughes tax reform was, in my opinion, much weaker than Cooper-Hughes. And it was unfortunate that a lot of people thought that it was an alternate to Cooper-Hughes. Really, Cooper-Hughes was tax reform; Agnew-Hughes was tax increase." Agnew admitted as much himself, further along in his farewell address: "With the insight that only experience affords, we now realize that the political compromises on the legislation were costly."

In terms of what he set out to do, then, Agnew failed on all counts. He did list other accomplishments, placing civil rights improvements next in importance to fiscal reform. He mentioned the legislature's repeal of an anti-miscegenation law that forbade marriages between Negroes and whites; a fair housing law; expansion of the public accommodations statutes; the establishment of an Advisory Committee on Human Rights to help develop legislation; the appointment of a Negro, for the first time, on the personal staff of a Maryland governor; and a Governor's Code of Fair Practices in employment in government and among businesses contracting with the state government.

Under examination, these accomplishments come to little. The repeal of the anti-miscegenation law was accomplished by the legislature on its own; it did not originate with Agnew. The fair housing law was later defeated in referendum. Agnew says in his farewell address, "Its subsequent defeat at referendum cannot diminish our pride in principled leadership. We acted out of conscience to right an historic wrong." What he called an act of conscience brought Agnew no credit from right or left. State Senator Clarence Mitchell, a black, charges Agnew with holding back on the issue:

> . . . there were those of us in the legislature who knew what the direction of the legislature was, the mood. We knew that we could get a stronger housing bill through. And he [Agnew] called us in ostensibly to get our ideas, but then he said, "This is the only bill that I'm going to get through." And we tried to point out to him that we had the votes for an even stronger bill—all he had to do was to give us the votes that he had promised—and we [would be] able to get enough to get it through. But he refused, and we ended up going through with the bill that he wanted. That was the only bill that he would endorse, even though the reality was that we could have gotten a stronger bill which would have given us a bigger tool to use in terms of persuading the black community that political involvement was a direction for answers to the problems that we faced.

The fact that the public accommodations law was a mere gesture, and required political courage to support it, can be seen in Agnew's attempt to defend it: "While the [public accommodations] law became academic because of federal legislation which intercepted it, the effort was tremendously important for it expressed Maryland's overt commitment to equal rights for all." Furthermore, this was again a legislative victory; all Agnew had to do was agree to sign it.

The appointment of a black, Dr. Gilbert Ware, to his personal staff, was an executive act that Agnew rightfully could claim full credit for—except that Dr. Ware had no influence or stature within the administration. Agnew seldom heeded his advice and turned to other staff members to handle such racial crises as those that developed at the Bowie and Maryland State campuses. The Code of Fair Practices, also an executive act, primarily mirrored changes in federal laws and the pressures of new court decisions. In any event, within a few months Agnew was being accused of not following up and enforcing the provisions of the code. Agnew often boasted that he appointed more blacks to state jobs than any previous governor, but his successor, Governor Marvin Mandel, after a year in office, boasted the same thing. Governor Mandel named blacks in about 4 per cent of his appointments, a record which beats Agnew's but is hardly anything to wave flags about.

Strangely enough, Agnew has always emphasized his role in civil rights changes and boasted of his accomplishments. ("Executive initiative in the field of human rights has, I believe, been without precedent," he said in the farewell speech.) It is, of course, a way to parry attacks of those who see a racist slant in his strong "law-and-order" positions. However, he seems to have a genuine sense of accomplishment in this field. But it is embarrassing to credit him with sincerity. His civil rights record, as demonstrated by his actions in the many crises that faced him, in his personal relations with black petitioners, including officials, and in the paucity of his executive accomplishments reveals that his sense of justice "in the field of human rights" is not only far below the expectations of blacks, but hardly keeps pace with the gains made around the nation.

Agnew's truncated term as governor will be remembered in retrospect for what it accomplished for Agnew, rather than for any legacy to the people of Maryland. When one considers his almost constant attention to his own political position outside Maryland, it is difficult to credit him with any great concern for the future of the state or its people. It is clear from the record that within a month after his inauguration as governor, Agnew's principal consideration was obtaining as much political prominence as he could during the build-up to the 1968 presidential election.

Vice-presidential candidates are not, of course, necessarily selected for the quality of their previous accomplishments. But the succession to the presidency of Harry Truman upon the death of F. D. Roosevelt, and of Lyndon Johnson upon the death of John F. Kennedy, have in recent years greatly increased public awareness of the importance of the vice-presidential role. Richard Nixon himself recounts, as one of his *Six Crises*, his own experience of the importance of the vice presidency during the first of Eisenhower's heart attacks. A Vice President, it has became clear, is a President-in-waiting. Nevertheless, in politics winning is first in importance. Serving in office is second in importance to winning. The reasoning is simple. To serve you must win first. And to win you must concentrate on the factors that mean the most to winning, not those which have to do with serving. Spiro T. Agnew was chosen as vice-presidential candidate by Richard M. Nixon because he best fitted that pragmatic principle. Not, perhaps, that Agnew would be the most help in winning, but that he would least interfere with Nixon's personal chance of winning.

Most voters, citizens and defenders of democratic systems have traditionally believed, in common with grammar school pupils in civics classes, that there exists in a democracy a competitive winnowing process that brings to the fore the best men, the most promising leaders, just as capitalism is supposed to drive down prices and encourage excellence in goods. That anyone can become President is not viewed with cynicism, as if the system were uncaring or haphazard. What people want to believe is that any American, regardless of the circumstances of his birth, can strive competitively toward that level of excellence from which national leadership may derive. And thus, to many Americans, the rise of Spiro T. Agnew can only be cause for wonder; if he is indeed the best that the system is capable of producing, are we to believe that he is also the best that the country can produce, or are we rather to doubt that the system is capable in these times, of working in a way consistent with the ideals of American democracy?

Index

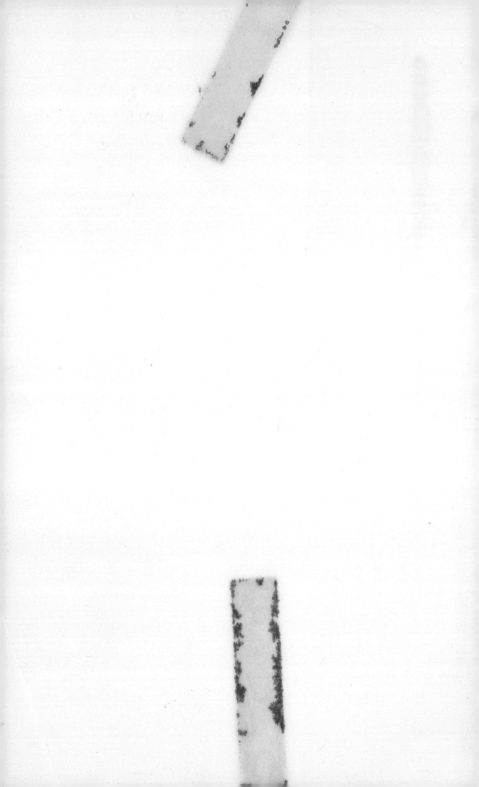